# Harry Thaw Hates Everybody

## by Laural Meade

Musical Arrangements by Curtis Heard

A Samuel French Acting Edition

SAMUELFRENCH.COM

Book and Lyrics Copyright © 2012 by Laural Meade

ALL RIGHTS RESERVED

Cover Design by Claudia Gómez
Photograph by Adrenaline-rest

CAUTION: Professionals and amateurs are hereby warned that *HARRY THAW HATES EVERYBODY* is subject to a Licensing Fee. It is fully protected under the copyright laws of the United States of America, the British Commonwealth, including Canada, and all other countries of the Copyright Union. All rights, including professional, amateur, motion picture, recitation, lecturing, public reading, radio broadcasting, television and the rights of translation into foreign languages are strictly reserved. In its present form the play is dedicated to the reading public only.

The amateur live stage performance rights to *HARRY THAW HATES EVERYBODY* are controlled exclusively by Samuel French, Inc., and licensing arrangements and performance licenses must be secured well in advance of presentation. PLEASE NOTE that amateur Licensing Fees are set upon application in accordance with your producing circumstances. When applying for a licensing quotation and a performance license please give us the number of performances intended, dates of production, your seating capacity and admission fee. Licensing Fees are payable one week before the opening performance of the play to Samuel French, Inc., at 45 W. 25th Street, New York, NY 10010.

Licensing Fee of the required amount must be paid whether the play is presented for charity or gain and whether or not admission is charged.

Stock licensing fees quoted upon application to Samuel French, Inc.

For all other rights than those stipulated above, apply to: SUBIAS, One Union Square West, #913, New York, NY 10003 Attn: Mark Subias.

Particular emphasis is laid on the question of amateur or professional readings, permission and terms for which must be secured in writing from Samuel French, Inc.

Copying from this book in whole or in part is strictly forbidden by law, and the right of performance is not transferable.

Whenever the play is produced the following notice must appear on all programs, printing and advertising for the play: "Produced by special arrangement with Samuel French, Inc."

Due authorship credit must be given on all programs, printing and advertising for the play.

**ISBN 978-0-573-69906-1**  Printed in U.S.A.  #29719

No one shall commit or authorize any act or omission by which the copyright of, or the right to copyright, this play may be impaired.

No one shall make any changes in this play for the purpose of production.

Publication of this play does not imply availability for performance. Both amateurs and professionals considering a production are strongly advised in their own interests to apply to Samuel French, Inc., for written permission before starting rehearsals, advertising, or booking a theatre.

No part of this book may be reproduced, stored in a retrieval system, or transmitted in any form, by any means, now known or yet to be invented, including mechanical, electronic, photocopying, recording, videotaping, or otherwise, without the prior written permission of the publisher.

### RENTAL MATERIALS

An orchestration consisting of **Piano/Vocal Score** will be loaned two months prior to the production ONLY on the receipt of the Licensing Fee quoted for all performances, the rental fee and a refundable deposit.

Please contact Samuel French for perusal of the music materials as well as a performance license application.

### IMPORTANT BILLING AND CREDIT REQUIREMENTS

All producers of *HARRY THAW HATES EVERYBODY* must give credit to the Author of the Play in all programs distributed in connection with performances of the Play, and in all instances in which the title of the Play appears for the purposes of advertising, publicizing or otherwise exploiting the Play and/or a production. The name of the Author *must* appear on a separate line on which no other name appears, immediately following the title and *must* appear in size of type not less than fifty percent of the size of the title type.

***HARRY THAW HATES EVERYBODY*** had its world premiere at the Los Angeles Theater Center, produced by the Indecent Exposure Theater Company and the City of Los Angeles Cultural Affairs Department. The production was directed by the author, with sets by Akeime Mitterlehner, lights by Cynthia Shiley, costumes by Linda Davisson, sound by John Zalewski, choral arrangements by Curtis Heard, musical direction by Steven Argila and choreography by Ken Roht. The cast was as follows:

| | |
|---|---|
| **EVELYN NESBIT** | Ana B. Gabriel |
| **STANFORD WHITE** | Chris Wells |
| **FLORENCE NESBIT** | Susan Rubin |
| **HARRY THAW** | Daniel T. Parker |
| **THE PIANIST** | Steven Argila |

## AUTHOR'S NOTES

Thank you for picking up a copy of *Harry Thaw Hates Everybody*. The play is structured in four acts, each patterned loosely after a different theatrical genre.

Act I is a vaudeville review.
Act II is a living newspaper.
Act III is a courtroom farce.
Act IV is an "avant-garde" collage.

The characters and events are based entirely in the capricious world of historical fact. The principals are quoted directly from the historical record throughout the play.

## CHARACTERS

The Ensemble:

**EVELYN NESBIT**, the famed beauty
**STANFORD WHITE**, her lover
**FLORENCE NESBIT**, her mother
**HARRY THAW**, her eventual husband
**A PIANIST**

Every one in this play is, at heart, a comedian. Please cast funny people.

The play can also be performed with two additional non-speaking roles:

**MIRABELLE**, servant to the ladies
**POIRE**, servant to the men

These characters fill out the visual thematic while functioning as stage hands. Resources permitting, they should be included. If this is not possible, in moments where their services are referenced, the lead players can look after themselves.

## SETTING

A lush, beautiful performance setting that suggests a late 19th Century theater. Chandeliers, potted palms, footlights, and an ornate proscenium with a grand red curtain. Patriotic red, white & blue bunting hangs throughout the house. Upstage, a decorative backdrop changes with each act. To the right and left of this backdrop are sitting areas in full view of the house. Each has a table and two chairs set for tea. Persian rugs, china and silver, fancy lamps. When the characters are not involved in the action, they take tea in these areas, occasionally coming on stage with a cup and saucer in hand.

As the audience enters the theater, Stanford and Harry sit upstage left, attended by Poire. Evelyn and Florence are having tea at the upstage right table. Mirabelle is not yet there.

All are dressed in gorgeous, formal, turn of the century attire. Perhaps the ladies' décolletage shows a bit more than propriety would allow.

Somewhere in the theater, a live pianist plays the music of the first decade of the 20th century: popular songs, sweet shanties, ragtime.

## A FINAL NOTE

It is suggested that the performance begin with the singing of the National Anthem of the United States of America, best led by our heroine Evelyn Nesbit.

## MUSICAL NUMBERS

All songs are authentic period pieces taken from original sheet music or recordings. Act I lyrics have been changed to accommodate the story.

Lyric and music credits appear at the end of the script.

### ACT I

*I Could Love a Million Girls*. . . . . . . . . . . . . . . .**STANFORD** and the **LADIES**

*Oh By Jingo* . . . . . . . . . . . . . . . . . . . . . . . . . . . . . **STANFORD** and **HARRY**

*Heaven Will Protect The Working Girl*. . . . . . . . . . . . . . . . . . the **ENSEMBLE**

### ACT II

*Who Are You With Tonight?* . . . . . . . . . . . . . . . . . . . . . . . . . . . . . **FLORENCE**

*Thee, Pamlico*. . . . . . . . . . . . . . . . . . . . . . . . . . . . . . . . . . . . the **ENSEMBLE**

*Your Mother is Your Best Friend*. . . . . . . . . . . . . . . **FLORENCE** and **EVELYN**

*Am I Not Fondly Your Own*. . . . . . . . . . . . . . . . . . . . . . . . . . the **ENSEMBLE**

### ACT III

*For The Sake of a Wife and Home/Why Don't They Set Him Free* . . . . . . **HARRY**

### ACT IV

*Broadminded Broad from Broadway*. . . . . . . . . . . . . . . . . . . . . . . . . . **EVELYN**

*No Man's Woman Now*. . . . . . . . . . . . . . . . . . . . . . . . . . . . . . . . . . . **EVELYN**

*(**EVELYN** is center stage. She is, as history tells us, impossibly beautiful, youthful, bright, and uniquely magnetic. Late teens to early twenties, a bit silly, but with an unlikely gravitas. She is also an utterly charming hostess - shaking hands, and ad-libbing fond greetings as she delivers:)*

## THE PROLOGUE – A GREETING FROM EVELYN

**EVELYN.** Hello hello and good evening to everyone. Thank you so very much for coming to the theater tonight…

I am Evelyn Nesbit. Born Florence Evelyn Nesbit, but I like just Evelyn better. I had quite a life. I believe that somewhere in the tumultuous wake of my experience, there's a message to be found. I guess. We'll just see.

Our story's got everything you could want in a good yarn. Beauty, sex, murder, money, true love…

A portion of the entire rigmarole is featured in the novel, motion picture, and musical play *Ragtime*, which I find flattering. However, at the end of his book, E.L. Doctorow writes, "Evelyn Nesbit lost her looks." Gentle guests, have I lost my looks? Have I? *(She ad-libs on this till the audience answers.)* Thank you!

I'm an author myself, you know. I wrote two books about my life. They're hard to find. In such great demand. Then again, I wrote the things about a hundred years ago and they've been out of print ever since. Time, time, time…

I suppose it's fair to call me obscure. An obscure historical figure. Now, anyway. That's all right. I've made my bed at this point!

**EVELYN.** *(cont.)* I lived the last 15 years of my life in Los Angeles. Died in Burbank of all places in 1967. It's true, folks. You stand warned - we're not going to be making any of this stuff up.

"Evelyn Nesbit lost her looks." Hmmf. The thing is, I believe I look unusually terrific. All things considered.

You know, they did *Ragtime* right here in _____. *(She names the city of the theater where the play is being performed.)* Over at the _____. *(She names whatever theater did* Ragtime *– certainly there will be one.)* Big musical fandango. I'm told I didn't play a very large part and that my song, although darling, did not reflect the complex magnitude of my story. *(She sings:)* "The Crime of the Century, la la la la la la…"

*(suddenly somber and far away)*

And here I am again. Dragged out for you all to see. I'm a muse for many people. Guess I'm not the only one who believes that somewhere in the tumultuous wake of my experience…

Well, *(coming back to her old self)* that brings us to the issue at hand. Indeed, on with my dirty little tale!

*(She returns to the playing area as the others join her.)*

*(***STANFORD** *radiates energy – huge, handsome, boisterous, loud, fun, and fast. Late middle age has only aided his charisma.)*

*(***FLORENCE***, early middle-aged, is a troubled woman. Handsome, Victorian, occasionally shrewd, occasionally hapless, a bit matronly, and slightly rough-hewn.)*

*(***HARRY***, late thirties to early forties, is wild-eyed, agile, excited, childish. Part fiend, part clown.)*

At the turn of the century in the year 1901, we all managed to bash in to each other in the most outlandish of ways. Stanford ended up dead, I ended up—well, suffice to say I'm dead too. We're all dead!

"Turn of the century." Sounds a bit familiar, doesn't it? I mean here we are with you, not long after the turn of another century. Wait till you hear what happened last time!

We couldn't come to a consensus, however, as to how our story should be told. So we decided to take turns and just slog through the whole darn thing. Everyone gets their own act.

**HARRY.** I wanna do my act now!

**EVELYN.** No Harry, Stanny starts us off.

**FLORENCE.** Mind yourself, Mr. Thaw. The night is young.

**STANFORD.** And so am I! Clear out, please…

*(The grand drape parts to reveal a backdrop that suggests a turn-of-the-century burlesque house: flowery details, racy cherubs.* **STANFORD** *is there, all bravado and daring. A boxing bell fires three loud bangs signaling the beginning of:)*

# ACT I
# STANFORD WHITE'S NEW YORK

**STANFORD.** Ladies and Gentlemen, MY NAME IS STANFORD WHITE! For my contribution to this evening's theatricals, I have been charged with providing the background of our social milieu and the characters therein. What you modern purveyors of dramaturgy might refer to as, ahem, exposition.

To keep the proceedings lively, I have prepared a variety of entertainments to be presented in the style of a vaudeville review. And what better way to begin than with a musical ode to MYSELF! Maestro!

*(The pianist plays as* **STANFORD** *sings in a charming rubato.)*

THE GILDED AGE, MY FRIENDS
IS NOT JUST ANY BELLE ÉPOQUE
GREAT PLEASURES COME TO THOSE WHO KNOW
JUST HOW TO WIELD THEIR...STOCK

YES TO THOSE OF US WITH WEALTH
THERE ARE NO LIMITS IN THE WORLD
MYSELF, I HAVE A PENCHANT FOR
THE COMPANY OF GIRLS

OH, I COULD LOVE A MILLION GIRLS, WITH EVERY GIRL A TWIN
I COULD LOVE A CHINESE GIRL, AN ESKIMO, A FINN
I COULD LOVE A RED-HAIRED GIRL, A GIRL WITH RAVEN CURLS
IN FACT I THINK THAT I COULD LOVE ABOUT A MILLION GIRLS...

*(The music kicks in to a quick tempo as* **EVELYN** *and* **FLORENCE** *enter to dance with him. A darling, if strange, chorus line.)*

**STANFORD.**
> BY DAY I AM THE ARCHITECT
> OF HIGH SOCIETY
> WE CURTSY AND CONDUCT OURSELVES
> WITH GREAT PROPRIETY
>
> BUT AFTER HOURS, DAMN THE RULES
> AND WHEN THE DAY IS DONE
> ROLL UP MY SLEEVES, ROLL DOWN YOUR DRAWERS
> THE WORK HAS JUST BEGUN!
>
> OH, I COULD LOVE A MILLION GIRLS, A MILLION GIRLS FOR ME
> I COULD LOVE A NATIVE GIRL FROM FAR ACROSS THE SEA

**LADIES.**
> HE COULD LOVE A GEISHA GIRL, A GIRL FROM ECUADOR

**STANFORD.**
> I LOVE THESE GIRLS SO GODDAMNED MUCH, LINE UP A MILLION MORE!
>
> LOOK UP WHEN YOU ARE IN NEW YORK
> EVERY OTHER SIGHT YOU'LL SEE
> IS AN ARCHITECTURAL WONDER
> WHOSE MASTERMIND IS ME
>
> LOOK DOWN, YOU'LL SEE A LOVELY GIRL
> BETWEEN EACH COLONNADE
> AND YOU CAN BET THOSE BUILDINGS WEREN'T
> THE ONLY THING I MADE!
>
> OH, I COULD LOVE A MILLION GIRLS, IT'S ALL I WANT TO DO
> SENORITAS FROM CHILE, SHERPAS FROM PERU

**LADIES.**
> HE COULD LOVE A BROWN-HAIRED GIRL, A GIRL WITH GOLDEN CURLS

**STANFORD.**
> I'M ON MY WAY TO LOVING JUST ABOUT A MILLION GIRLS!
>
> I'M NOT THE ONLY MAN OUT THERE
> TO WOO YOUNG GIRLS WITH GUMPTION
> THE RULING CLASSES DO IT WITH
> CONSPICUOUS CONSUMPTION

THE KINGS OF CULTURE LOVE IT
ASTOR, VANDERBILT AND TATE
I EVEN SHARED A SPREE OR TWO
WITH SEVERAL HEADS OF STATE!

OH, I COULD LOVE A MILLION GIRLS, GIVE EVERY GIRL A TWIN
A MADEMOISELLE FROM GAY PAREE, A FRAU FROM OLD BERLIN

**LADIES.**

HE COULD LOVE A MILLION GIRLS, WE TELL YOU MARK HIS WORDS

**STANFORD.**

BRING ON THE SCOTS, THE POLES, THE CZECHS. WELL HELL, BRING ON THE KURDS!

*(He slows to a lascivious rubato.)*

AND SO MY FRIENDS, I SING A SONG
OF BEAUTY, GREED, AND PLEASURE
ANOTHER DAY OF HO-HUM WORK
FOR A CLASS WHOSE JOB IS LEISURE

WE'LL LET OUR HUMBLE DRAMA
TELL THE FATE OF RICH AND POOR
BUT THE MORAL OF THE STORY IS…
WE'RE ALL A BUNCH OF WHORES!

*(Tempo kicks back in with panache.)*

OH, I COULD LOVE A MILLION GIRLS, A MILLION GIRLS COULD I!
I LURE THEM IN TO MY EMBRACE AND PROMISE THEM THE SKY
I COULD LOVE A MILLION GIRLS, IN FACT I THINK I DID
HOW MANY LADIES WILL IT TAKE TO SATISFY MY ID?!

**LADIES.**

HOW MANY LADIES WILL IT TAKE…

**STANFORD.** *(big finish)*

TO SA-TIS-FYYYY… MYYYY—

*(HARRY, restless and annoyed, has taken a gun out during the previous and begun to wave it around. Just at this moment he points it at STANFORD's head and shoots. Bang bang bang!)*

**STANFORD.** AHHHH! Goddamn it Thaw! That was nearly the end. You've ruined my number!

**HARRY.** What? That's what really happens! The song plays, I shoot you in the head.

**STANFORD.** You shoot me during the reprise in your act. This is my act! Good God. Now they're all going to know what happens!

**HARRY.** No, no. The song was going on too long. I did you a favor.

**STANFORD.** No applause, nothing. The entire opening – ruined!

**HARRY.** So finish. Finish the number!

**STANFORD.** NO.

**HARRY.** Yes! YOU'RE THE ONE WHO'S YELLING. FINISH IT!

**STANFORD.** *(singing annoyedly)*
HOW MANY LADIES WILL IT TAKE TO SATISFY MY ID?!
There! Let's move on.

**HARRY.** You got your ending. Does any one want to applaud now?

*(The audience does.)*

**STANFORD.** Ladies and Gentlemen, please hold your applause till the end of the act.

*(HARRY steals a bow.)*

Goddamn it, Thaw. We're moving on!

*(POIRE has produced a lectern/podium on wheels for STANFORD. The others retire to their tables.)*

**STANFORD.** You must excuse the folly of my colleague. I can guarantee with great certainty that outbursts will continue to occur as the evening wears on…

Where were we...? Ah yes - exposition! Let me now paint for you the idyllic backdrop against which our sordid tale unfolds.

In the grand tradition of American oratory, for our next novelty I have prepared a brief lecture with accompanying visual aids about...

*(Lights dim. The upstage backdrop doubles as a screen for Stanford's slide show.)*

*(a slide appears reading:)* "Manahatta!" as the natives endearingly called it. Or *(another slide reading:)* "The Island that Stanny Built!"

*(As the lecture progresses,* **STANFORD** *wheels and careens all over the playing area with his podium. He bangs on it, leans on it, rides it like a shopping cart.)*

*(An old timey slide of the New York City skyline)*

Yes it's the great, teeming megalopolis of New York City. Everything the world has to offer by way of people, culture, possessions. Not so much a place, as a focus of illusion. *(another slide of NYC)* I think I'll be the first to coin this sentiment when I say, "New York City – My Kind of Town!" And here's another I thought of this morning, "King of New York!" That would be me, my friends.

*(A slide reading "1901!")*

The year is 1901 and we find ourselves present at the very dawn of the Twentieth Century. The early morning celestial air is thick with transformation, innovation, and the NEW. By the time it's all over, no social institution is left unrevolutionized...

Our attention turns first to changes in *(a slide reading:)* "Attitudes!" I'm thrilled to note that during this era New Yorkers begin to painstakingly wrest themselves away from *(an image of pure Victorianism)* the sentimental frippery of Victorian prudishness. Slowly, exquisitely, both the hoi-polloi and plebian begin to

**STANFORD.** *(cont.)* embrace *(an image of folks dancing and drinking)* a looser, more hedonistic set of social rules. Skirts shorten by an entire inch, and music begins to syn-co-pate.

*(A slide reading:)* "Technology!" The good ol' Industrial Revolution is in full mechanized swing. Invention thrives. Gothamites catapult themselves in to the intoxicating embrace of each stunning new advance: *(slides of each)* the telephone – hello, the phonograph – la-dee-dah, electricity – ahhh!, the horse-less carriage – heaven. *(a slide reading)* "Bigger, better, faster, louder" are the *mots du jour* here. This suits me fine, as those mots are practically my middle name.

*(A slide reading "Stanford Bigger Better Faster Louder White")*

Anyway, what's next? *(a slide reading)* "Profit!" Ah yes – Money! It is the Gilded Age, after all, and as the title implies just about everything in fair N-Y-C is dusted with a veneer of Gold. *(image of coins and cash)* Wealth abounds, for those who can afford it. And poverty rears its hungry head for almost every one else. Now what flabbergasts me is not that some people were filthy rich but that so many people were filthy poor! *(a slide of a rag-wearing mob)* I had no idea, for example, *(a slide of an aerial map)*, until I bothered to look over the back fence, that some of the 5th Avenue fiefdoms I created were butted right up against rows of squalid tenement slums. Yuck!

But then again, why bother to look when you're too busy having what—?

*(A slide reading "Pleasure!")* That's right, pleasure of course. New York in 1901 loved its shindigs! And if you're going to party, you need a place to do it. And thus – New York's many and infamous Gentlemen's Clubs. *(a slide of the The Riders Club)* This is one of my designs – the Riders. The Ride-hers... *(a slide of The*

*Player's Club)* This is another – The Players. For actors. Ever spent a boozy evening with a bunch of actors? Well then, you know... *(a slide of a club room with gentlemen present)* Oh, the Gentlemen's Club. Cigars and sherry in one room, *(a slide of a club room with both ladies and gentlemen present)* Roxanne and Sherry and Marylou in another. Ah, Mmmmaryloooo...

*(A slide of rich old farts at a party –* **STANFORD** *is circled)*

Ah! Speaking of parties - here I am with some of my natty clientele at a big splashy soiree. That's Mamie Stuveysant-Fish down in the corner there. Rich old bag, and one of the weirdest women I know. But my god she had money. They all did. In fact, let's flip back a few slides cuz it bears repeating. *(slide returns to "Profit!")* WE ALL HAD MONEY. And these New Yorkers are delighted to show it! To lead the loaded charge. And who's leading them? Me, of course!

You see, Ladies and Gentlemen, my relation to the ruling class, Manhattan's fashionable mob was practically galvanic! I designed their homes, I defined their tastes, I encouraged and enabled their wildest, most opulent dreams. Let's face it – I taught those goddamned people, and this confounded city, how to be rich!

*(Studying the slide)* A fine bunch, each with their merits but, betwixt you and I, some of the meanest people on the planet. And each of them with a sack of gold about 10,000 times bigger than yours.

*(A slide of an early American flag)* Well, as one of my literary friends so aptly put it, "Inequality is as dear to the American heart as liberty itself."

And now, back to me! I mean, back to Manhattan!

*(A slide reading:)* "In summation!" If in the fearsome metropolis of New York City *(a slide of a scary NYC street scene)* amid a time of intense transformation, citizens

**STANFORD.** *(cont.)* both rich and poor find themselves in a world ever more shaken by practically schizophrenic change, then my architectural creations are indeed the salubrious anodyne of aesthetic charm I have always believed them to be. I close with some of the loveliest gifts Manhattan and I offer...

*(A slide of Penn Station)* Pennsylvania Station – a wrought-iron tribute to the romance of travel; *(a slide of Judson Church)* Judson Memorial Church – rising as a gracious rebuke to the uncivilized spirit of the buildings around it; *(a slide of Madison Square Garden)* the original Madison Square Garden – an Eden-like ode to the pursuit of pleasure; *(a slide of Washington Arch)* Washington Arch – buoyant gateway launching Fifth Avenue on its steadfast course; *(a slide of some funny misplaced turn-of-the-century pornography)* the majestic Doric column in Brooklyn's *(he finally notices)* Good God! That's not a Doric column at all... *(he signals to flip ahead)* Well, you'll excuse me! *(a slide of yet more porn)* Oh my! These seem to be for another lecture I was to deliver later on. *(another – they're getting increasingly risqué)* Ah! What I did on my summer vacation! *(a slide of The Tiffany Building)* Here we go. The Tiffany Building with its intrepid thrusting pilasters – never mind. Back to the porn! *(back to porn)* Ah, my baby sitter! *(another – a naked goddess Diana)* My archery instructor! *(a lone woman pleasuring herself)* Good night Nurse! Speaking of archery, bulls-eye!

*(He wheels his podium over to the backdrop and gets uncomfortably close to the most delicate part of the photo. After a moment, he finally remembers he's not alone.)*

Hell, if we could find my keys we'd drive out of here! Well, then...Thus concludes my oratory in the grand American tradition! Hmmm. Next, next, what's next...

*(Lights come up as he returns the podium to the care of* **POIRE**, *then sets himself center stage.)*

Oh, yes. Speaking of weird, mean rich people – allow me to introduce the weirdest, meanest richest of them all. Ladies and Gentlemen, the next member of our dramatis personae, Harry K. Thaw.

**HARRY.** Of Pittsburgh!

*(Harry joins him center stage as the pianist vamps. They sing.)*

**STANFORD & HARRY.**
FANCY MANNERS, DRESS, AND LINGO
ARE DECEIVING, OH BY JINGO

**STANFORD.**
TAKE THIS YOUNG MAN FOR EXAMPLE
HIS APPETITE FOR MAYHEM'S AMPLE

**STANFORD & HARRY.**
NEXT TO JOHN, PAUL, GEORGE, AND RINGO
I/HE GET/S MORE KICKS, OH BY JINGO

**HARRY.**
AND EVEN THOUGH I'M FLUSH
IT'S ALWAYS THE BUM'S RUSH!

*(The music stops. They do a little talk-patter.)*

**STANFORD.** You get the bum's rush, eh? Your filthy lucre should have opened any door in town.

**HARRY.** Oh I made sure it did.

**STANFORD.** How so?

**HARRY.** When a shopkeeper wouldn't let me in his store, I bought a car and drove it through the window!

**STANFORD.** And when the best gentlemen's club in New York turned you down—

**HARRY.** I ponied up cash for a horse and rode it through the front door!

**STANFORD.** Giving new meaning to the phrase-

**BOTH.** Hi-Ho Silver!!!

*(The music kicks back in.)*

**STANFORD & HARRY.**
> OH BY GEE, BY GOSH, BY GUM, BY JAY
> OH BY JINGO, STAY OUT OF MY/HIS WAY

**HARRY.**
> BAD BOY OF THE JET SET WORLD

**STANFORD & HARRY.**
> DIRTY LAUNDRY ALL UNFURLED

**STANFORD.**
> HE'S HATED BY THE RICH OF OLD MANHATTAN

**STANFORD & HARRY.**
> FROM QUEENS TO THE ISLE OF STATEN!
> BY JINGO, OH BY GOSH, BY GUN

**HARRY.**
> I'LL NEVER BE NEW YORK'S FAVORITE SON

**STANFORD & HARRY.**
> STILL WE ALL CARRY ON SINGING
> OH BY GEE, BY GOSH, BY GUM, BY JUM, BY JINGO
> BY GEE, HE'S/I'M AS BAD AS HE/I CAN BE!

**HARRY.**
> MY LOVE OF PROVOCATION
> CAN'T MATCH HIS REPUTATION

**STANFORD.**
> HE CLAIMS I USE COERCION
> TO BED PUBESCENT VIRGINS

**HARRY.**
> "KING OF NEW YORK," OH BY JINGO
> ACTING LIKE SOME RANDY DINGO

**STANFORD.**
> HIS COUNT AS OF LATE
> IS THREE-HUNDRED SEVENTY-EIGHT!

*(***STANFORD*** laughs. The music stops again. More patter.)*

**HARRY.** That's right! According to my notes, White has ruined 378 young ladies! I'm gonna prove it!

**STANFORD.** You won't get a single peep out of a single girl.

**HARRY.** How's that?

**STANFORD.** I kept my shenanigans on the oh so private.

**HARRY.** What's the point of pawing a pretty girl if no one sees you do it?

**STANFORD.** Because you know what kind of light made every one of those girls her prettiest?

**HARRY.** What kind?

**STANFORD.** *(slowly)* The dark, Thaw. The deepest blackest dark…

*(**HARRY** shivers, obviously titillated. It all gets extra creepy for a moment.)*

**STANFORD & HARRY.**
OH BY JOE, BY GOSH, BY GUM, BY GEE

**STANFORD.**
OH, BY JINGO HE'S OBSESSED WITH ME!

**HARRY.**
I'VE BUILT MY LIFE 'ROUND ONE COMPLAINT
THAT WHITE HERE ACTS WITH NO RESTRAINT

**STANFORD.**
BUT YOU'VE SEEN YOUR SHARE OF FLAGRANTE DELINGO
NOT TO MENTION CUNNI-LINGO…

*(He turns the words in to a raunchy demonstration.)*

**HARRY.** Stop it! Stop iiiittt!!!

**STANFORD & HARRY.**
OH BY JINGO, OH BY JOSH, BY JUTZ
BY JOVE WE HATE EACH OTHER'S GUTS!

SO WE ALL CARRY ON SINGING
OH BY GEE, BY GOSH, BY GUM, BY JUM, BY JINGO
BY GEE, HE'S AS BAD AS HE CAN BE!

*(The song finishes with a big bang. **HARRY** tries to steal all the bows.)*

**STANFORD.** Thank you for your kind attention, Ladies and Gentlemen. But please hold your applause until the end of the act! Sit down, Thaw!

**HARRY.** Well, when's my act?!

**STANFORD.** Third act's your act. If you stick around after intermission, dear audience, you'll, ahem, see it... Next, next...what's next...? Oh, yes, the ladies and their humble beginnings. For their introduction, I have prepared an extraordinary MELODRAMA!

Intuit the mounting tension! Witness reports from the principles! Scene!

*(The others have entered and strike a heavily posed, old-time tableau. Sappy music from the piano. Everyone hams it up.)*

The run-down living room of the Nesbit home. No kitchen sink - they can't afford it!

**EVELYN.** Oh mother, here we are in Pittsburgh: struggling but content. At least we have love!

**FLORENCE.** Not so fast, Evie – I'm sorry to report your father has died and left us penniless!

**EVELYN.** Daddy! Not my daddy!

**FLORENCE.** You were always his favorite. Now we have nothing nothing nothing!

**EVELYN.** And younger brother Howard seems to grow weaker with every passing day.

**HARRY.** *(coughs, as* **HOWARD**...*)*

**FLORENCE.** Here it is, the turn of a grand new century, and yet I find myself society's pawn. The only things I know how to do are raise children and clean house!

**ALL THREE.** WHAT SHALL BECOME OF US?!

**STANFORD.** All stratagems fail. Soon our desperate family migrates to Philadelphia. Scene!

*(They strike another tableau!)*

**EVELYN.** Oh mother, here we are in Philadelphia: poor and destitute, living on the wrong side of the tracks.

**FLORENCE.** Children, I have found us work at a local department store!

**EVELYN & HARRY.** A department store?

**FLORENCE.** Me as saleswoman, Howard as a cashboy and you Evelyn as a lowly stockgirl.

**HARRY.** *(coughs, as* **HOWARD**...*)*

**STANFORD.** Soon the Nesbit family is hard at work. For this one instance I shall portray the respected Philadelphian painter John Storm. Scene!

*(Tableau!)*

Oh miss, do you have these wool underpants in a size 42 — My God, you're pretty! An ideal mix of girlish purity and brazen mystique. Won't you pose for me?!

**EVELYN.** I guess so...

**FLORENCE.** Evelyn, my darling! I must voice my doubts about the propriety of such work.

*(***STANFORD** *pulls out a big wad of money.* **FLORENCE** *grabs it and stuffs it down her corset.)*

But then again, looks like food on the table to me!

**STANFORD.** After just twelve months in Philly, Evelyn's modeling career was growing by leaps and bounds. Thus, her mother announced, scene!

*(Tableau!)*

**FLORENCE.** I know: let's try New York!

**EVELYN.** Oh, mother WHAT SHALL BECOME OF ME?!

**HARRY.** *(coughs, as* **HOWARD**...*)*

**FLORENCE.** Who knows? But you'll get paid! Come Evelyn, we'll be late.

**STANFORD.** Within weeks of their arrival in New York—

*(New York tableau!)*

Young Evelyn was posing, day and night, for distinguished painters—

*(Painting tableau!)*

Sculptors—

*(Sculpting tableau!)*

And photographers!

*(Photographic tableau!)*

**FLORENCE.** *(alarmed by* **EVELYN***'s increasingly gleeful and risqué poses)* Oh Evelyn. What shall become of you?

**EVELYN.** Who knows? But I'm getting paid!

**STANFORD.** As the glittering girl model of Gotham, her dazzling countenance was seen everywhere, including magazines read by members of the theatrical profession. Scene!

*(Tableau!)*

**HARRY.** I'm a member of the theatrical profession. I'd like to offer you a featured part as a Spanish dancer in the hit musical *Floradora*. You'll be a Broadway star!

**FLORENCE & EVELYN.** Gasp!

**STANFORD.** Thus ends our sketch, truly rendered and a mere portend of things to come!

*(All hoot and holler as* **EVELYN** *does a brief Spanish dance.)*

**ALL.** Olé!

**STANFORD.** You're too kind, too kind, but please hold your applause till the end of the act! And now, my dear friends, we near the crux of my enthralling exposition. What you purveyors of modern dramaturgy, and I know you're out there, might call the inciting incident of the entire tale. Evelyn and I...meet. And then, Harry... And then...

*(He stops for a moment, forgetting where he is, wondering what went so very wrong. He rubs his soon-to-be-shot forehead.)*

...Once more, I have chosen to dramatize these events through the medium of song. A finale, if you will. Won't you join in if you know the refrain?

*(Throughout this song,* **FLORENCE**, **STANFORD** *then* **HARRY** *manhandle, paw and roughhouse* **EVELYN**. *Humorous, but mean.)*

**FLORENCE.**
>A SWEET YOUNG GIRL OF JUST SIXTEEN
>TOOK BROADWAY'S WORLD BY STORM
>HER MOTHER DEAR WITH WORRISOME FEAR WAS RENT
>"THE THEATER WORLD IS NOT SO NICE
>A CARNIVAL OF VICE
>SOME GUIDANCE, I THINK, WOULD BE HEAVEN-SENT"
>
>AND JUST LIKE THAT, A FAN CLUB FORMED
>RICH MEN WITH SAGE ADVICE
>A RAY OF HOPE AMIDST THE HEATHEN SWIRL
>"IF ONE OF THEM SHOULD SHOW CONCERN
>I'M SURE I'D NOT THINK TWICE…"

**EVELYN.** *(spoken)* You mean if some rich old lobster wanted to tell us what to do – you wouldn't think twice?

**FLORENCE.** Sure I would. And then I'd think – where do I sign us up?!

>*(sings)*
>
>FOR HEAVEN WILL PROTECT THE WORKING GIRL!

**STANFORD.**
>HER DEAR OLD MOTHER'S HOPE CAME TRUE
>FOR SOON THE YOUNG GIRL MET
>A MAN WHO ON HER SAFETY SEEMED INTENT
>HE LOOKED A LITTLE BIT LIKE NERO
>ACTED ALL THE HERO
>SO SHE SUPPOSED HE WAS A PERFECT GENT
>
>HE SHOWED HER ALL THE CITY HAD
>JUST LIKE A SUGAR-DAD
>AND LAVISHED HER WITH ERMINE, MINK AND PEARL
>"YOU ARE AN ANGEL IN MY LIFE!
>JUST DON'T TELL MY WIFE…"

**EVELYN.** *(spoken)* You're married?! Oh well, that's good. Means you'd never try anything, right? Right?

*(A beat. Would he?)*

**STANFORD.**
>OH, HEAVEN WILL PROTECT THE WORKING GIRL…

**HARRY.**
> ABOUT THIS TIME THERE ALSO WAS
> ANOTHER FELLOW WHO
> WAS TAKEN WITH HER BEAUTY, GRACE AND CHARM
> HE FOLLOWED HER IN SECRECY
> HER BENEFACTOR TOO
> WHO HE WAS SURE JUST MEANT TO DO HER HARM
>
> HE SIGNED HIS NOTES "MONSIEUR MUNROE"
> AND WRAPPED HIS GIFTS IN CASH
> HIS REAL NAME HE NEVER WOULD UNFURL
> STILL USING HIS STRANGE ALIAS
> HE SENT A LIQUORED DEMITASSE!
>
> *(**POIRE** offers **EVELYN** a fancy drink and flowers stuffed with cash.)*

**POIRE.** *(spoken)* Courtesy of Mr. Munroe.

> *(During **EVELYN**'s little tirade, **FLORENCE** grabs all the cash and drinks the booze.)*

**EVELYN.** Who does this guy think he is?! Take it all back! I'm sixteen - and not for sale! Right, mama?

**FLORENCE.** *(hiccupping)* Ab-solutely!

**HARRY.**
> OH, HEAVEN WILL PROTECT THE WORKING GIRL...

**EVELYN.**
> STAND BACK VILLAINS
> HEAR MY CRY:
> MY HONOR YOU'LL NOT PLY!
> ALTHOUGH YOU ARE AN ARTIST OR AN EARL
> YOU MAY TEMPT THE UPPER CLASSES (AND MY MOTHER APPARENTLY)
> WITH YOUR ANONYMOUS DEMITASSES
> BUT, HEAVEN WILL PROTECT THE WORKING GIRL!

**ALL.**
> OH, HEAVEN WILL PROTECT THE WORKING GIRL!
> THE WORKING GIRL!

*(Three bangs from the boxing bell signal the end of the act. Lights slowly dim as* **STANFORD** *finally takes his applause.)*

**STANFORD.** Bring it on folks. End of the act! Vene vidi vici. And what a job, too. Superb storytelling! I think I discharged my section beautifully. Fantastic...

*(Lights back up on* **EVELYN** *alone.)*

**EVELYN.** My my, what a charmer. Certainly you can see why I fell for Stanny. And he hasn't changed a lick. If anything, he's gotten younger. I think we all have, in our deaths. Come to think of it, Stanford really was a big ol' pig when I met him. 30 years my senior, fat, grey, dripping with gin.

But he was so attentive and clever. And the parties he threw! A connoisseur of delight.

*(She sings absentmindedly)* "The Crime of the Century, la la la la la..."

**EVELYN.** My mother is up next. By the by, I never thought to wonder if she wanted my stardom for herself…

I miss my mother. *(She re-thinks)* I miss the idea of my mother.

Anyway, on with the show!

*(Lights change as a settee is moved center stage and a new backdrop is revealed: a large rendering of the front page of an old and yellowing newspaper. Throughout the act, with the ring of a bell at the top of each new scene, the masthead ["New York Post" etc.], headline ["Chorus Cutie Scores Swank Hotel!" etc.] and date change to follow the story as it unfolds. A large black and white photo – an actual snapshot of a key moment in the live scene – also changes.)*

*(***FLORENCE*** enters. She bravely attempts to present a gracious demeanor, but years as a middle-class woman out of her league in high society has left her over-whelmed*

*and easily rattled. In spite of this, she does manage to pepper her story-telling with occasionally effective irony or charming sarcasm.)*

*(Whenever she provides narration the* **PIANIST** *accompanies her with ragtime music.)*

*(With great aplomb the other characters come and go from their tea tables as the scenes dictate. The whole act moves with urgent speed and detailed specificity. Ragtime music begins as the lights come up on:)*

# ACT II
# FLORENCE GETS DOWN TO BUSINESS

**FLORENCE.** How do you do. My name is Evelyn Florence Nesbit. Welcome to Act II.

In this next part of the story so very many things happened – all of it terribly upsetting and still a confusion. I thought I'd rely on reports from the press for a definitive version of who did what with who. As it turns out, the stories only told half-truths. So we're going to show you everything the papers didn't say – in the form of a living newspaper.

Ladies and Gentlemen, you take a look at who *really* did what with who and decide for yourself the *why*...

I pick up the story several months *after* our introduction to Stanford, when he suggested, insisted actually, I take a trip a home to Pittsburgh. The paper told all about our new residence upon my return, but not a word about the man behind it all...

*(A bell rings. The newspaper details and photo change to "New York Post, December 1901." The headline reads:)*

**ALL.** "Chorus Cutie Scores Swank Hotel!"

**STANFORD.** Dear Evelyn will be well taken care of. In fact, I'll show her things she's never dreamed existed.

**FLORENCE.** Sir, your generosity is a constant source of comfort. Little Howard writes that he is happy and healthy away at school, thanks to you. I can't imagine how we'll ever repay you—

**STANFORD.** Evelyn's charming company has already been payment enough. In fact, upon your return I'm moving you both into The Wellington Hotel.

*(He snaps his fingers and* **MIRABELLE** *[if the production is using the servant characters] appears at the ladies' tea table.)*

**FLORENCE.** The Wellington? We couldn't—

**STANFORD.** On my account of course.

**FLORENCE.** Bless you, Mr. White. You are our greatest and only friend in New York. what would we do—

**STANFORD.** Adieu.

**FLORENCE.** Add-do?

**STANFORD.** *Adieu.*

**FLORENCE.** Ah! Adieu…

**STANFORD.** *(to the* **PIANO PLAYER***)* This little girl's mother has gone away and left her care to me.

**PIANIST.** Good God!

**STANFORD.** Champagne for you, Kittens?

**EVELYN.** Yes, please Stanny.

**STANFORD.** *(He pours.)* Just one now. Will you miss your mother?

**EVELYN.** Gosh no! She manages to make herself so very present at all times.

**STANFORD.** Like a babbling brook.

**EVELYN.** Hmm?

**STANFORD.** Nothing, Kittens. Go on.

**EVELYN.** I'll miss her by the end of the week, certainly. But for now, it'll be fun to be on my own. With you! *(jumping into his lap)* I feel so grown up!

**STANFORD.** You sure do…

**FLORENCE.** It went on like that for several hours. Treats, laughter, harmless repartee about the subjects that pleased her most.

**EVELYN.** Books, kitty-cats, swings—

**STANFORD.** I have a red velvet swing.

**EVELYN.** You do?

**STANFORD.** I'm going to put you in that swing—

**EVELYN.** And push me high!

**STANFORD.** Higher and higher...

*(During **FLORENCE**'s song, **STANFORD** beckons **EVELYN** to drink up. She does so and quickly passes out. He carries her behind the newspaper backdrop, thinking the audience can't see them back there. **FLORENCE** sings. She has her hands full pulling off the song and doesn't pay attention to much else.)*

**FLORENCE.**

BILL BOUNDER WAS A ROUNDER
JUST AS ROUND AS HE COULD BE
HE ROUNDED ALL AROUND THE TOWN
WITH EVERY GIRL HE'D SEE

AT LUNCHEON HE HAD GENEVIEVE
AT DINNER HE HAD JO
AND THEN HE HAD SOMEBODY ELSE
EACH EVENING AT THE SHOW

A YOUNG SOUBRETTE, BUT OLD COQUETTE
SAID I REMEMBER YOU
I'VE SEEN YOU OUT WITH MOLLY
AND I'VE SEEN YOU OUT WITH SUE

BUT WHO ARE YOU WITH TONIGHT, TONIGHT?
WHO ARE YOU WITH TONIGHT?
WHO IS THE DREAMY, PEACH AND CREAMY
VISION OF SWEET DELIGHT?

IS IT YOUR LITTLE SISTER, MISTER?
ANSWER ME, HONOR RIGHT
WILL YOU TELL YOUR WIFE IN THE MORNING
WHO YOU ARE WITH TONIGHT, TONIGHT?
WHO ARE YOU WITH TONIGHT?

*(During the song, behind the backdrop, **STANFORD** and **EVELYN**'s shadow can be seen in silhouette. He is clearly on top of her, pants down. She is not moving.)*

*(Finally, he sees their shadow and quickly gets up, slapping **EVELYN**'s face to rouse her. They come out from behind, straightening themselves up, just as **FLORENCE** finishes. Seems what happened then, has happened again now. Uncomfortable all around.)*

**FLORENCE.** Mr. Thaw, I believe it's your line.

**HARRY.** Mr. Munroe!

**FLORENCE.** What?

**HARRY.** I'm incognito!

**FLORENCE.** Fine. Mr. Mun—

**HARRY.** Miss Nesbit, allow me to finally introduce myself – Mr. Munroe at your every service.

**EVELYN.** *(recovering but disheveled)* Ah. the secret flower-sender.

**HARRY.** You received my gifts then?

**EVELYN.** Always – and at the strangest places. Beauty parlor, dentist, the alley when I'm taking out the trash. I'm beginning to think you might be following me.

**HARRY.** *(kissing the hem of her dress)* The whole world follows you, Evelyn.

**EVELYN.** You are…quite the flatterer. Well, you'll excuse me.

**HARRY.** Why does your mother permit you to see that beast Stanford White?

**EVELYN.** I beg your pardon?

**HARRY.** That beast Stanford White!

**EVELYN.** I heard you.

**HARRY.** Well?

*(Evelyn turns to **FLORENCE**, who wears a small, stoic smile, then to **STANFORD** who also remains aloof.)*

**EVELYN.** Mr. White is as nice as he can possibly be, especially to my family. He's exceedingly thoughtful, more so than most people.

**HARRY.** We'll see what we can do about that. Good day, Miss Nesbit.

**EVELYN.** Good day…

*(A bell rings as the newspaper changes to "New York Press, April 1902." The headline reads:)*

**ALL.** "Nesbit's Rose in Bloom!"

**FLORENCE.** Evelyn's career blossomed. In private, she and Stanford carried on what seemed to me a perfectly innocent friendship. In public, a big Broadway hot shot put a new musical together just for her, *The Wild Rose*.

(**EVELYN** *does a brief "wild rose" dance.*)

Then the big Broadway hot shot's wife divorced him and named Evelyn as a defendant in the suit. The gossip columns said my wild rose was spreading her petals all over New York. But, as it turns out, Stanford was the one with his fingers in the dirt.

**STANFORD.** *(into the phone at his tea table)* I need flowers, candy and cards sent to the Wellington, the Hartford, the Hilton, the Beckwith, the Standard, the Royalton, and *(catching the eye of a female audience member)* the *(he names the theater where the show is taking place)* _____ Theater, third row on the aisle...

*(He ad-libs a lascivious flirtation with her.)*

**FLORENCE.** Evelyn couldn't stand it. After six months or so she began to accept some of the offers she was receiving from other wealthy gentlemen about town. Unfortunately, the one who most interested her wasn't wealthy at all - he was an actor. A young fellow named John Barrymore.

*(A bell rings as the newspaper changes to "New York Times, May 1902." The headline reads:)*

**ALL.** "2-bit Ham Woos B-way Hoofer!"

**FLORENCE.** Yes, *the* John Barrymore.

**HARRY.** I'm John Barrymore now.

**STANFORD.** Evelyn, I'd like you to meet John. John, this is Evelyn Nesbit.

**HARRY.** *(kissing her hand)* Jack, please.

**EVELYN.** Wow.

**HARRY.** I'm studying to be an actor. I've seen you in *The Wild Rose*. You're divine.

**EVELYN.** Gee.

**HARRY.** A quivering pink poppy in a golden, wind-swept space.

**EVELYN.** I love you.

*(They laugh, embrace, flirt...)*

**FLORENCE.** He sent her violets. She laughed at his jokes. One thing led to another.

*(...and flounce right in to **FLORENCE**.)*

**EVELYN.** Mother?!

**FLORENCE.** Where have you been all night?!

**EVELYN.** With Jack Barrymore.

**FLORENCE.** No!

**EVELYN.** Yes! We drank too much and I decided to stay at his room to sleep it off.

**FLORENCE.** Sleep it off, huh?

**EVELYN.** Don't think that anything else happened because it didn't!

**FLORENCE.** Oh, Evelyn!

**STANFORD.** Jack Barrymore, huh? I should have seen it coming.

**HARRY.** Stanford.

**STANFORD.** Mr. Barrymore.

**HARRY.** Hello, Evelyn.

**EVELYN.** Jackie!

**STANFORD.** I suppose you're wondering why I've called us all here.

**HARRY.** Evelyn, will you marry me?!

**EVELYN.** Why yes!

**STANFORD.** This is an outrage! Good God, will the two of you come to your senses!

**EVELYN.** I'm in my senses. I think Jack is very amusing and I like him very much. Why shouldn't we be married?

**STANFORD.** Preposterous! What will you live on?!

**HARRY.** Love!

**STANFORD.** Ah! His whole family's queer, Evelyn. And they're ACTORS! Stop this charade.

**EVELYN.** No!

**STANFORD.** (*to* **HARRY**) You - out out out!

**FLORENCE.** I don't like the little pup either.

**EVELYN.** I'll marry Jack if I want to and neither of you can stop me. No one's going to stop me!

**FLORENCE.** My daughter had become very aware of her power over men. And I realized that I was simply no longer a match for her.

**HARRY.** I'm not Jack Barrymore any more.

**FLORENCE.** Thank you.

(*A bell rings. The paper changes to "New York American, August 1902." The headline reads:*)

**ALL.** "Evelyn Trades Toe Shoes for Grad Cap!"

**FLORENCE.** Again, the story didn't say a word about the man behind it all…

**STANFORD.** I'm sorry, Kittens.

**EVELYN.** So am I, Stanny. You're the only one for me.

**FLORENCE.** Ah-hem.

**EVELYN.** For us.

**STANFORD.** (*producing a brochure*) That may very well be, but just to be safe I've arranged for you to go to school.

**FLORENCE & EVELYN.** School?

**FLORENCE.** (*reading from the brochure*) "Located in the great outdoors of Pompton Lakes, New Jersey, The Pamlico School for Girls offers young ladies educational guidance, instruction in the fine arts, blah, blah, rates for room, board and tuition are—"

**STANFORD.** Don't worry, Mother, I'll pay the bills.

**EVELYN.** Oh Mother, "room and board." That means I'll live in New Jersey?

**STANFORD.** What do you say, Kittens?

**EVELYN.** Well, if you want me to.

**STANFORD.** Without question. You start in a few months. Florence, I've arranged everything with the headmistress. She's a good friend of mine.

**FLORENCE.** Mm-hmm.

**STANFORD.** Farewell, my lovely. I'll be round to see you when I can.

**EVELYN.** Good-bye, Stanford. Thanks, I think.

**FLORENCE.** So Evelyn set her sights on Pamlico. Just before she made her exit, a certain Mr. Munroe succeeded in procuring a dinner date.

**HARRY.** And I've seen your show forty times. *(kissing the hem of her dress for each day)* On the 2nd and the 3rd. I skipped the 4th, but the saw the matinee and the late show on the 5th—

**EVELYN.** Mm-hmm.

**HARRY.** Furthermore, I am not who you believe me to be!

**EVELYN.** Oh?

**HARRY.** I am, in fact, Harry Kendall Thaw!

*(**EVELYN** yawns.)*

Of Pittsburgh!!

**EVELYN.** Ah! Quel surprise.

**HARRY.** One final question – will you marry me?

**EVELYN.** OH – no! Alas, I start seventh grade next week…

**FLORENCE.** So off Evelyn went, not giving another thought to Mr. Thaw. Stanford, acting the concerned patron, continued to pay our bills. And my daughter, for the first time since the death of her dear father six years prior, went to school. But even then, the courting never stopped.

*(The four characters begin singing with the **LADIES** standing in front, **GENTLEMEN** in back. Soon after the song starts the men begin shoving to get closer to **EVELYN**. By the end of the tune, **FLORENCE** has been tossed out of the way.)*

**ALL.**
>SORROW WITH BITTER TEARS
>THIS MAY COME IN FUTURE YEARS
>YET, A JOY TO US THOU'LL BE
>THEE, PAMLICO, ONLY THEE

*(A bell rings. The newspaper reads "New York Evening Journal, April 1903." The headline:)*

**ALL.** "Super Soubrette's Parochial Peril!"

**FLORENCE.** And then, one day...

**EVELYN.** Mother, come quick. I don't feel so well. Mama...

*(She faints.)*

**FLORENCE.** Evelyn. Evie? Evie?!

*(**FLORENCE** grabs the phone on her table and dials. The phone on the gentlemen's table rings. **POIRE** offers it to **STANFORD** who is in the audience flirting with another woman.)*

Stanford! Answer your phone!

**STANFORD.** I'm busy!

**FLORENCE.** Busy doing what?

**STANFORD.** Having a baaahhhth...

**FLORENCE.** What was I to do? Stanford was nowhere to be found.

*(She dials again. **POIRE** offers the phone to **HARRY**. He answers.)*

**HARRY.** Harry K. Thaw here.

**FLORENCE.** Mr. Thaw, this is Florence Nesbit.

**HARRY.** What a pleasant surprise. How is your merry ray of sunshine?

**FLORENCE.** She's not very well, I'm afraid. I can't seem to reach Mr. White—

**HARRY.** Arrogant, virgin-ruining, fat hunk of meanie fat!!

**FLORENCE.** Uh-huh... Evelyn's in serious trouble - medically speaking - and I, uh, well, Mr. Thaw...

**HARRY.** I'll dispatch my surgeon to Pamlico right away.

**FLORENCE.** My goodness, how is it you know she's there?

**HARRY.** I make it my business to know a lot of things, Mrs. Nesbit. Don't worry, I'll take care of Evelyn.

(**HARRY** *runs to* **EVELYN**, *scoops her up, and plops her down center stage on the settee.*)

**HARRY.** My angel. Don't worry now. Harry's here. My boo-fuls. Harry fix boo-fuls right up. Boo-fuls love Harry.

**EVELYN.** Uh, yeah.

**HARRY.** Boo-fuls say thank you, Harry.

**EVELYN.** Thank you, Mr. Thaw.

**HARRY.** Harry. HARRY!

**EVELYN.** HARRY!

**HARRY.** (*flatly*) Good.

(*A bell rings as the paper reads, "New York Tribune, May 1903." The headline proclaims:*)

**ALL.** "Thaw Treats Nesbit to European Respite!"

**FLORENCE.** At this point Mr. Thaw had what seemed like a viable idea: a recuperative European trip for dear Evelyn – and her mother. By both their accounts the congeniality between Evie and Stanford had gone cold.

**STANFORD.** Brrrr. Evelyn who?

**FLORENCE.** So off we sailed. Harry paid for everything and Stanford, still acting the gentleman, gave us a letter of credit should anything go wrong. Thank goodness for that…

**HARRY.** Garçon, my wife ordered snails, not pigeon! And furthermore, there's a fly in my soup.

**EVELYN & FLORENCE.** Your wife?!

**HARRY.** Doing the backstroke!

**FLORENCE.** Mr. Thaw, your soup is fine.

**HARRY.** No, it's not. This whole meal is a shambles. Why should Harry K. Thaw of Pittsburgh have to put up with such nonsense?!

*(He pitches an outrageous, frightening fit. He gasps, sputters and spits, ending up prostrate.)*

**EVELYN.** Harry, I ordered pigeon! What's wrong with you?

*(He fixes an audience member in the eye as **EVELYN** helps him up.)*

**HARRY.** What are you looking at? Take your eyes off my wife!

**EVELYN.** You'll have to forgive him. Too much money and not enough love.

**FLORENCE.** He had outbursts in Oslo, rages in the Rhineland, and paroxysms in Paris. But just as easily as he would weep and sputter, he could be honey-sweet.

**HARRY.** I'm so sorry, Boo-fuls. I, I, I...love you so much. How ever will you forgive me? Clothes? Furs? Jewels?

*(He dangles a spangly bauble in front of her. She grabs it.)*

**EVELYN.** Well, I suppose that would be a pretty good start.

*(Then another for **FLORENCE**.)*

**HARRY.** One for you too, mother.

*(She takes it, is momentarily delighted, then quickly recovers.)*

**FLORENCE.** And on it went. More outbursts, more gifts. What was I to do? Retreat seemed the only option.

**EVELYN.** But mother, we've just gotten to Paris – there's still so much I want to see. And Harry, well, he can be awfully sweet when he wants to.

**FLORENCE.** And an animal when he doesn't. We still have Stanford's letter, sweetheart. Let's make use of it.

**EVELYN.** Stanford. Ha! A lot of good he did us.

**FLORENCE.** Evelyn, come to your senses!

**EVELYN.** I'm in my senses. I'll stay with Harry if I want to and you can't stop me. No one's going to stop me!

**FLORENCE.** Then I'm going back to London – where I can at least be understood when calling for help!

**EVELYN.** Good! Bon Voyage! That means "please leave!"

**FLORENCE.** Seeing no other option, I did. And as soon as I was gone:

**HARRY.** Evelyn!

**EVELYN.** What?!

**HARRY.** You MUST marry me.

**EVELYN.** Oh, Harry NO. My career, you see. I'm planning a triumphant return to the stage.

**HARRY.** It's that philandering White, isn't it?

**EVELYN.** No.

**HARRY.** It is! How can you continue to pine after him?! I want to marry you, Evelyn. I've wanted a pretty virgin as a wife since I can remember. And you're the one!

**FLORENCE.** He badgered her for three days and nights until my poor daughter made, as she described it off the record, the greatest, most terrible, and costliest mistake of her life.

**EVELYN.** We just can't be married, Harry! If you want a virgin, that is, because, well, you see, um, Stanford and I—

**HARRY.** A-HA!

*(He clutches his chest in a fit of apoplexy and falls to the floor, again.)*

**FLORENCE.** He sobbed, he raged. He said he forgave her, but she knew he didn't. Eventually they returned to me in London, both the worse for wear. Evelyn, of course, told me none of what had happened. We weren't exactly speaking by then.

*(**HARRY**, bored, runs interference between them.)*

**HARRY.** *(to **EVELYN**)* Your mother wants to go back to New York.

**EVELYN.** I want to stay!

**HARRY.** *(to **FLORENCE**)* Evelyn wants to stay.

**FLORENCE.** Well I'm leaving!

**HARRY.** *(to **EVELYN**)* She's leaving.

**EVELYN.** On whose dime?

**FLORENCE.** *(to* **EVELYN***)* Stanford White, that's who! *(to* **HARRY***)* Stanford Stanford Stanford!

*(***HARRY** *starts to go off again, but* **EVELYN** *soothes him.)*

**EVELYN.** *(glaring at* **FLORENCE***)* All right, Sugar, all right...

*(As* **FLORENCE** *continues,* **EVELYN** *and* **HARRY** *waltz, with suggestions of an Apache dance.)*

**FLORENCE.** With me out of the picture, Thaw was free to unleash his most erratic behavior. He became stranger in Holland, stranger still in Germany. In Austria, sequestered with Evelyn at a castle in the middle of nowhere, he reached a new height of...derangement.

*(***EVELYN** *falls. Did* **HARRY** *trip her? After an uncomfortable beat, a bell rings and the paper changes. "New York Press, October 1903." The headline reads:)*

**ALL.** "Nesbit's Toes Touch American Terra!"

**FLORENCE.** The papers failed to mention that Stanny cornered her immediately upon her return.

**STANFORD.** Kittens!

**EVELYN.** What?!

**STANFORD.** Could it be you? You look older and wiser by years.

**EVELYN.** Hello to you too, Stanny. How have you been?

**STANFORD.** At sixes and sevens. Too much of everything. Work, wine—

**EVELYN.** Women.

**STANFORD.** Touché. How is your mother?

**EVELYN.** You'd know better than I. We haven't spoken since she left Europe. Or should I say, since she left me.

**STANFORD.** What?

**EVELYN.** Oh, Stanny. It was awful, a nightmare.

**STANFORD.** Good lord, child. Tell me everything.

**FLORENCE.** And she did. The papers didn't get an account of Evelyn's tale, but Stanford and his lawyer were treated to an earful.

*(He deposits her somewhere vulnerable and sets himself comfortably on the settee. As the questioning continues,* **STANFORD** *takes an increasingly prurient interest while* **EVELYN** *grows increasingly flustered.)*

**STANFORD.** How long had you been in Europe before you were left alone with one Harry Kendall Thaw?

**EVELYN.** Well, we'd already seen the Black Forest, Eiffel Tower, *(singing a bit sadly)* London Bridge was falling down—

**STANFORD.** When did the said Thaw begin to exhibit perverted behaviors?

**EVELYN.** He was always an oddball, but the pervert business didn't kick in till after Mama left—

**STANFORD.** Was there anyone watching the two of you?

**EVELYN.** Bellhops, scullery girls. No one I knew—

**STANFORD.** Did you and the said Thaw play any dirty little games?

**EVELYN.** I don't know if you'd call it a game, but there was this thing he liked to do with his fork—

**STANFORD.** How about role playing? Dress up?

**EVELYN.** We posed as a married couple. It was Harry's idea, but after a while I kinda liked it—

**STANFORD.** Strike that! ...Was there a swing involved?

**EVELYN.** Oh Stanny, that's your toy, not his—

**STANFORD.** Strike that too! ...Did you dance for him?

**EVELYN.** Sure. Get enough liquor going and it's 5-6-7-8—

**STANFORD.** Then he gave you a little slap?

**EVELYN.** I wouldn't call it that—

**STANFORD.** And a little harder?

**EVELYN.** Yes—

**STANFORD.** And a little harder?

**EVELYN.** Well, uh—

**STANFORD.** When did the said Thaw first begin to abuse you?

**EVELYN.** In Austria. He was so calm at dinner, but then midnight rolled around and Mr. Hyde showed up —

**STANFORD.** And he reared back and struck you?

**EVELYN.** You could say that.

**STANFORD.** Did he cuff you? Slap you?

**EVELYN.** Um…

**STANFORD.** Grab you? Thrash you?

**EVELYN.** He hit me.

**STANFORD.** How much?

**EVELYN.** Stanny, this is getting strange. I thought you were going to help.

**STANFORD.** How much?!

**FLORENCE.** Evelyn, please! Just tell us what happened.

**EVELYN.** *(she pauses, summons her strength, then slowly and deliberately)* Thaw came in to my room unannounced. He grasped me by the throat and tore the bathrobe from my body. I saw by his face that he was in an excited condition. His eyes were glaring and he had in his right hand a leather whip. He seized hold of me and threw me on the bed. I was powerless and attempted to scream, but Thaw placed his fingers in my mouth to choke me. Then, without any provocation, he began to inflict upon me severe and violent blows. I begged him to desist, but he refused. He acted like a demented man. So brutally did he assault me that my skin was cut, bleeding, and bruised. He threatened to kill me. And then… well, he… *(she trails off, unable to say what happened next)* It was nearly three weeks before I was sufficiently able to get out of bed and walk.

*(to* **STANFORD***)* Later he said he did it because of us. He blamed… you.

**STANFORD.** Strike that.

*(There are three slow sad dings and a loaded pause. The paper changes to "New York Morning Sun, December 1903." The headline reads:)*

**FLORENCE.** "Pixie Does Dixie." She swore to Stanny that she would never see Harry again. She moved from hotel to hotel in an effort to escape the watchful gaze of his many detectives. As usual, she told me none of what had happened. I read that she made her triumphant return to the stage in *A Girl From Dixie.*

*(***EVELYN** *does a Dixie-type dance, crossing from* **STANFORD** *to* **HARRY**.*)*

When her eighteeth birthday rolled around, I assumed she'd spend it with her old pal Stanford. But no.

Ladies and gentlemen, imagine my surprise when the papers reported that not only did she spend her birthday with Harry, but that she was moving in to his hotel? That she was, in essence, going to live with him?

*(A bell rings. The paper changes to "New York Herald, January 1903." The headline reads, "Evie Hangs Hat at Harry's.")*

**FLORENCE.** Why? Why would she do that?

When I received an offer of marriage from a family friend back in Pittsburgh, I took it. And left New York and Evelyn for good. Why? Why would I do that?

I look back on it all now and I think – Oh hell's bells, what did they want from me?!

*(The* **PIANIST** *plays as* **EVELYN** *enters for a tongue-in-cheek duet.)*

**FLORENCE & EVELYN.**
 YOUR MOTHER IS YOUR BEST FRIEND AFTER ALL
 SHE'S ALWAYS THERE TO HELP YOU WHEN YOU FALL
 WHEN YOUR DAYS ARE DARK AND DREARY
 MOTHER DEAR DOES NOT GROW WEARY
 JUST A WORD AND SHE COMES QUICKLY AT YOUR CALL

**EVELYN.**
 I WAS SICK AND BROKEN HEARTED
 ALL MY FORTUNE SEEMED TO FLEE
 FROM MY FRIENDS SO SADLY PARTED
 STILL DEAR MOTHER WELCOMED ME

**FLORENCE & EVELYN.**
> YOU'LL FIND LOTS OF FRIENDS AS THROUGH THIS WORLD YOU ROAM,
> BUT THERE'S NO FRIEND LIKE YOUR MOTHER DEAR AT HOME;
> THOUGH HER BROW'S ALL LINED WITH CARE,
> AND THERE'S SILVER IN HER HAIR,
> YOUR MOTHER IS YOUR BEST FRIEND AFTER ALL.

> (**FLORENCE** *bustles around with* **MIRABELLE**, *making to leave. All are immediately agitated.*)

**EVELYN.** I can't believe you're moving back to Pittsburgh.

**FLORENCE.** I can't believe you're still seeing that crackpot.

**EVELYN.** Don't go.

**FLORENCE.** Stay here and watch you make the biggest mistake of your life? No thank you.

**EVELYN.** Well what else do you suggest?! Stanford has lost all interest in me. I don't have any friends or any job prospects other than sweating it out in some chorus. And how much longer can that last?

Harry pays the bills. Handsomely I might add. He's apologized and I believe him. In fact, when he's in his right mind, he shows me every kindness that, well, that a mother would.

**FLORENCE.** Pshaw!

**EVELYN.** Look Mama, this set-up is what every girl in every show on Broadway wants. It just comes with a few eccentricities.

**FLORENCE.** Good-bye, Evie.

**EVELYN.** Maybe I will marry him —

**FLORENCE.** Heaven help us.

**EVELYN.** — and we'll move back to Pittsburgh too! And live in a much bigger house than yours!

**FLORENCE.** I wish you the best of luck—

**EVELYN.** I'm joking. Please stay.

**FLORENCE.** – because I think you'll need it.

**EVELYN.** Please...

*(A bell rings. The paper changes to "New York World, 1904." The headline reads:)*

**ALL.** "Harry Presses as Mother Regresses!"

**FLORENCE.** According to the papers, the entire next year found Evelyn evermore courted by Harry. I wouldn't know for certain – once I was back in Pittsburgh, our communication ceased entirely.

*(***HARRY*** rushes to ***EVELYN***. The newspaper headline changes briefly to:)*

"Harry's Harried Over Harrowing Heroine."

**HARRY.** You drive me even crazier than I normally am!

*(The title changes again...)*

**FLORENCE.** "Broadway Babe Sets Mad Harry's Heart Aflame."

**HARRY.** But I am only as crazy as you drive me because you are beautiful as I am driven crazy!

**EVELYN.** That actually makes sense to me.

**FLORENCE.** I read in one column that the couple had made a public scene when they refused to register at a hotel as husband and wife. We were still safe on that end. I fantasized that if she ever did agree to marry him, Stanford would try to dissuade her.

*(with great camp and terrific feeling...)*

**STANFORD.** Evie!

**EVELYN.** What?!

**STANFORD.** Don't marry Harry! Don't do it!

**EVELYN.** Leave me alone. Imagine the consequence if he found us together!

**STANFORD.** I knew it! He scares you. He scares everybody!

**EVELYN.** If only you knew his good side.

**STANFORD.** I'll do anything I can to torpedo this marriage. I'll dig up dirt on him that'll make the city editors swoon.

**EVELYN.** Don't!

**STANFORD.** You can't possibly love him.

**EVELYN.** What do you know of love?

**STANFORD.** Plenty.

*(They kiss. Passionately, sloppily, unmercifully.)*

Now you're mine again, and you'll do as I say. Just like before.

**EVELYN.** Just like before? Stealing around in the middle of the night. Waiting for telephone calls that never come. Dying of shame when your society friends smile with their mouths but laugh with their eyes!

**STANFORD.** Don't think about those things.

**EVELYN.** You know it's the truth. And I can't do it any more! Neither should you.

**STANFORD.** Don't think about me!

**EVELYN.** I do think about you. I think about you because... I love you!

**STANFORD.** Ah!

**EVELYN.** But I can't love you! My heart belongs to him. Farewell...

**STANFORD.** Go if you must. But if you ever want me, know that I will always want you.

*(He tries to kiss her again. She grandly rebuffs him.)*

Good-bye, Evie.

**FLORENCE.** That was a scene based on a scene between Joan Collins and Ray Milland from *The Girl In The Red Velvet Swing*, a big technicolor movie made in 1956. In actuality Stanford had a very different take on the subject of marriage for Evelyn. Tell 'em what you really said.

**STANFORD.** Good riddance! She was foolish and headstrong, and will thus be out of all temptation!

**FLORENCE.** In the other corner, Harry Thaw never let up.

**HARRY.** Evelyn!

**EVELYN.** What?!

**HARRY.** My life will have been a meaningless flop unless you agree to become my wife. Please darling, won't you say YES?

*(He drops to his knee and sings.)*

YOU, YOU, REIGN IN THIS BOSOM
THERE, THERE, HAVE YOU A THRONE
YOU, YOU, KNOW THAT I LOVE YOU
AM I NOT FONDLY YOUR OWN?
YES, YES, YES, YES!
AM I NOT FONDLY YOUR OWN?

*(**STANFORD** joins in singing with **HARRY**. **FLORENCE** speaks over them.)*

**FLORENCE.** Then Harry brought in the big guns - his mother. Although she was repelled by the idea of her beloved son marrying an actress, she did say just what my poor girl apparently needed to hear: "My son is very much in love with you, Evelyn, and I wish you would marry him. We would welcome you in to our family as a wife and a daughter."

**HARRY & STANFORD.**
THEN, THEN, E'EN AS I LOVE YOU
SAY, SAY, WILL YOU LOVE ME?
THOUGHTS, THOUGHTS, TENDER AND TRUE, LOVE
SAY, WILL YOU CHERISH FOR ME?
YES, YES, YES, YES
SAY, WILL YOU CHERISH FOR ME?

*(**FLORENCE** joins them. Poor **EVELYN** is caught in the middle of all three.)*

**HARRY, STANFORD & FLORENCE.**
YES, YES, YES, YES!
YES, YES, YES, YES!
YES, YES, YES, YES–

**EVELYN.** All right! Yes! *(tenderly)* I'll marry you...

**HARRY.** *(flatly)* Good.

*(He drops her hand and exits as the boxing bell clangs three times, signaling the end of the act.)*

**FLORENCE.** *(also leaving)* Well. There you have it, folks. Just a little light reading and not bad if I do say so myself...

**STANFORD.** *(chasing after her)* I'll be the judge of that, Florence! Ladies and Gentlemen, we will now take a brief intermission wherein I will give my fellow players their notes...

*(**EVELYN** follows them out to the strains of ragtime as the lights hit black.)*

## -INTERMISSION-

## HARRY THAW HATES EVERYBODY CONTINUES...

*(The audience enters to find the ladies at their tea table on the right, the gentlemen at theirs on the left.* **EVELYN** *comes center stage and greets the house.)*

**EVELYN.** Welcome back, everyone! Delighted to see you again...

Wasn't mother's front page something? You really do read the damnedest things in newspapers. Some people can't get enough...

As luck would have it, they had just figured out how to print photographs when my story hit its climax. Nobody had her picture in the paper as much as little ol' Evelyn. People stopped me on the street just to touch me! For years.

Do you think I would change any of what happened to me? If you guessed no, you'd be right...

Who's next? Harry, of course. We're about to be married! You know, I wore black to my own wedding. True. And I should warn you, days like this always make me cry...

*(The boxing bell sounds three times as the curtain and lights come up on:)*

# ACT III
# HARRY TAKES OVER

*(The pianist provides a dour version of "Here Comes the Bride" as the foursome make a classic marriage ceremony arrangement.* **FLORENCE** *holds a bridesmaid bouquet and* **STANFORD** *holds a ring pillow.* **EVELYN** *wears a black tulle veil.* **HARRY** *stands next to her with an excited look on his face.* **MIRABELLE** *and* **POIRE** *place subtly silly flower arrangements about. The new upstage backdrop suggests an outdoor trellised courtyard.)*

*(The wedding march ends and* **HARRY** *lifts* **EVELYN**'s *veil for the consummating kiss. Just as their lips are about to touch...)*

**HARRY.** Finally, a chance to act in my own defense! How I have managed to play along with these charades is beyond me!

**STANFORD.** Thaw...

**HARRY.** *(singing, cruelly lampooning)* "I Could Love a Million Girls, Your Mommy is Your Best Friend...!" *(He blows a big raspberry)* Damn nothing but SLANDER!

**STANFORD.** Thaw, just what are you up to?

**HARRY.** Now, Ladies and Gentlemen, in an effort to prove myself the true victim of this entire circumstance, I have taken the opportunity presented to me—

**STANFORD.** Harry K. Thaw!

**HARRY.** By the fact that you are all my captive audience—

**STANFORD.** Thaw!

**HARRY.** What?!

**FLORENCE.** What are you DOING?

**EVELYN.** Please don't excite him.

**STANFORD.** I knew this was going too smoothly.

**HARRY.** I admit that at first I planned to go along with the whole set-up, but after a while I got another idea in my head.

*(He pulls on the upstage rigging and a new backdrop comes crashing down - a plain muslin with the words "HARRY THAW IS INNOCENT" hand-painted in messy red letters.* **HARRY** *bows in front of it until he gets some applause.)*

**HARRY.** Thank you, thank you. I made it myself.

**STANFORD.** Harry Kendall Thaw, what is the meaning of this?!

**HARRY.** Shut up, White! I did your bit, with a smile on my face, no less. Now you'll do as I say.

*(From his table area,* **HARRY** *pulls out a pile of new scripts. The covers read "SURPRISE ACT III BY HARRY K. THAW.")*

Ladies and Gentlemen, I'm sure none of you will object when I inform you we will be following a NEW SCRIPT for my section.

**STANFORD & FLORENCE.** We object!

**HARRY.** I wasn't addressing you!

**EVELYN.** Hold on, let's see what he's done.

**HARRY.** Thank you, Evelyn. A little filler music, please.

*(The* **PIANIST** *plays something funny while* **HARRY** *hands scripts out to everyone, tech staff included.)*

**HARRY.** Now, let me preface what will undoubtedly be the most authentic information you will hear tonight by making a few points. First and—

**STANFORD.** *(referring to a line in the new script)* What the hell is this?!

**HARRY.** Stanford White, one more interruption and I'll kick you out of my act.

**STANFORD.** Done!

*(He throws his script down and strides toward the theater door.)*

**HARRY.** Which will leave you no recourse to address anything I might have to say about you.

**STANFORD.** AH!

*(He appeals to a woman in the audience he was flirting with earlier.)*

Would you like me to stay, dear?

*(She'll probably say yes.)*

Well then. He seems to have us, doesn't he?

**FLORENCE.** By the chestnuts.

**EVELYN.** Mother!

**HARRY.** That's more like it. As I was saying: first and foremost, I am forced to note that I hold myself beyond reproach.

**EVELYN.** Of course you do.

**HARRY.** Secondly, the interviews I have prepared are calculated to make every one else like me as much as I like me.

**STANFORD.** Propaganda!

**HARRY.** Exactly. Finally, given that I'm a fan of good entertainment, I have also prepared a medley of song to be sung by me and an interpretive dance to be danced by me.

**FLORENCE.** Is this a joke?

**STANFORD.** Yes.

**HARRY.** There. Well. I think things are going swimmingly so far.

**EVELYN.** Harry, I thought some of what you had put together for us was a real pip. Maybe you should reconsider—

**HARRY.** *(raising his fist to her)* NO!...

*(He sees the others seeing this.)*

**HARRY.** Evelyn, I pose one simple request to you in my entire life and you refuse me.

**EVELYN.** Of course. Right. Well then, let's begin.

*(Her acquiescence is not lost on **FLORENCE** and **STANFORD**.)*

**HARRY.** Thank you. More filler music, please...

*(**HARRY** gestures to **POIRE** and together they produce from backstage what looks like a tall box on wheels. It is covered in a sheet.)*

Crescendo, please!

*(He rips the sheet off to reveal a terribly makeshift witness stand. Shabby, crooked, too small for anyone to sit in comfortably. He again bows until he gets some applause.)*

Thank you, thank you. I made it myself.

*(He seats the ladies at chairs he has directed **POIRE** to put in the playing area.)*

Now, Florence you are here, and Evelyn you'll start here.

**STANFORD.** What about me?

**HARRY.** Why don't you...go blow it out your ass!

**STANFORD.** That would be a charming thing for all of us to sit through. Me blowing it out my ass for the third act. That's some re-write, Thaw—

**EVELYN.** Stanny, just let him alone.

**STANFORD.** But he...oh, Evelyn...

*(He sits.)*

**HARRY.** Thank you. I'd like the lights to change now. Something dramatic.

*(They change.)*

Now, page one everybody.

**FLORENCE.** We're ready, for criminy sake!

*(**HARRY** reads from his script with great drama and flourish-filled conviction – fancying himself the grandest barrister-orator-hero ever…\*)*

**HARRY. Ladies and Gentlemen, my original trial established the fact that I suffer from Dementia Americana! A type of insanity, which is not so insane, wherein a man whose home has been violated believes himself right in exacting any revenge. However, because that trial devolved into a public lynching, the world never got to see how Demented my Americana truly is! Now, for this trial I shall be my own counsel—**

STANFORD. You know what they say about a man who represents himself?

HARRY. Do not complete that joke.

STANFORD. What are you gonna do? Shoot me?

*(He lampoons **HARRY** waving his gun around.)*

**HARRY. WE'LL BEGIN by questioning the mother of my fair young flower. I call to the stand Mrs. Evelyn Nesbit!**

FLORENCE. *(climbing on to the stand)* It's actually Florence. Florence Holman. I got married in the last act, remember?

HARRY. Yes, yes, but I thought it was Evelyn Florence.

FLORENCE. It is, but I just go by Florence.

EVELYN. I go by Evelyn.

HARRY. I know that, but for the purposes of the court—

FLORENCE. She's Florence Evelyn. I'm Evelyn Florence, but I haven't gone by that for years.

EVELYN. Now she's just Florence, and I'm just Evelyn.

HARRY. Evelyn Florence?

EVELYN. No, Evelyn.

FLORENCE. But I occasionally call her Florence.

STANFORD. But you're Florence.

FLORENCE. Evelyn, actually, but not legally. Evelyn Florence.

EVELYN. Wait, I'm Evelyn Florence.

---

\* Note: **Bold** sections of text indicate passages from Harry's revised script.

**FLORENCE.** Only for the stage, dear. Florence Evelyn—

**HARRY.** Stop it! The script! Stick to the script!

**FLORENCE.** Well, all right. I only wanted to clarify for the court.

**HARRY.** Are you making fun of me?!

**FLORENCE.** No, Mr. Thaw. Let's please continue.

**HARRY.** Fine. *(He searches his script)* Ah yes. **Mrs. Evelyn Nesbit, would you please state your full name for the court.**

**FLORENCE.** Florence Holman!

**HARRY.** Stop that! **Mrs. Nesbit, please describe your situation during Evelyn's early youth.**

**FLORENCE.** Well, we lived in Pittsburgh, a perfectly happy little family until my husband died—

**HARRY.** From the script, Florence! Good God!

**FLORENCE.** Oh. Yes…

*(At this point, **FLORENCE** finally looks at the script. She does her best, but the stress of a last-minute acting assignment gets the better of her. She mispronounces a variety of words, large and small. Some are noted, but the actress can do what she will throughout. **HARRY**, for the most part, is oblivious – caring more about his performance than hers.)*

Ahem…**During Evelyn's early youth we enjoyed a typically boor-gee—**

**EVELYN.** Bourgeois.

**FLORENCE.** — **lifestyle. My husband, however, pursued a profession renowned for its fraudoo – fraw-dull—**

**EVELYN.** Fraudulency.

**FLORENCE.** — **that of a lawyer.**

**HARRY.** Who argued cases against my family!

**FLORENCE.** Once. And he lost!

**HARRY.** Neener neener! Continuing: **Did the late Mr. Nesbit make any provisions for you or his children, in the event of his death?**

**FLORENCE.** No.

*(He gestures madly to her script.)*

**No, he didn't.**

Mr. Thaw, we've introduced this information already.

**HARRY.** I don't care! If I want to stress that your deadbeat husband tried to ruin my family and then succeeded at ruining yours, I will! Continuing: **How long did it take you to realize you had a valuable commodity in your daughter?**

**FLORENCE. Not long. Within months, we freely accepted gifts and currency from that notorious type of vulture: artists.**

**HARRY. Did you also accept my assistance without question?**

**FLORENCE. Yes, for by then I had become accustomed to exploiting the bewitching booty—**

**EVELYN.** Beauty.

**FLORENCE. —of my daughter.** I can't believe this!

**HARRY. As evidenced by the fact that although you travelled to Europe on my generosity, you also took support from White in the form of a letter of credit. Mrs. Nesbit, please tell the court what you did with that letter of credit in Europe.**

**FLORENCE. I bought fancy French lin-ger-ree.**

**HARRY.** *(pronouncing it correctly)* Lingerie!

**STANFORD.** Underwear?!

**FLORENCE.** All right, so I did. But that's not all! I used it to get home. To get away from you!

**HARRY.** So you did leave us?

**FLORENCE.** Yes!

**HARRY. Which brings me to my next point, Why did you *abandon* your daughter in Europe?!**

**FLORENCE.** That's it.

*(She throws her script down, climbs off the stand, and heads for the theater doors.)*

**HARRY.** Florence, I was very well behaved for you. We can't have complete anarchy, can we?

**EVELYN.** Please, Mama.

*(She slowly returns, entirely perturbed.)*

**HARRY.** Why did you *abandon* your daughter in Europe?

**FLORENCE.** Because you were deranged.

**HARRY.** Florence—

**FLORENCE.** You were violent and rude.

**HARRY.** From the script!

**FLORENCE.** Because I was afraid Evelyn was turning toward your affections…

**HARRY.** Finish.

**FLORENCE.** — and away from those of my generous benefactor, Stanford "Meal Ticket" White.

**HARRY.** In other words, had I supported you in the same style, you would have stayed.

**EVELYN.** Is that true?

**FLORENCE.** Well…

**HARRY.** Course it is. Even though I spent just as much on you as he did.

**FLORENCE.** And then took it away whenever the mood struck. At least with White the checks were regular.

**STANFORD.** Florence that's terrible.

**FLORENCE.** Well, from the pot to the kettle—

**HARRY.** Lastly, during my murder trial did you receive money from my family for agreeing not to testify against me?

*(She doesn't respond.)*

Florence?

**FLORENCE.** Yes.

**HARRY.** How much?

**FLORENCE.** Fifty thousand dollars.

**HARRY.** In today's currency, one and one quarter million dollars.

**EVELYN.** Mother, how could you...

**FLORENCE.** You found your benefactor - but in the bargain, I lost mine!

**HARRY. There you have it, Ladies and Gentlemen.** *(with great contempt)* **A money-grubbing mother, a ne'er-do-well father, fancy French underwear. By the time poor Boo-fuls came to me, I was her only chance for survival. Mrs. Nesbit, you may step down...!**
Great work, Flo. You read beautifully.

*(She leaves the stand.)*

**FLORENCE.** *(to EVELYN)* Baby. I'm so sorry. I assumed you... understood...

**HARRY.** Wonderful. This is going along really well. A perfect set-up for the dance I have prepared.

*(Screwy orchestral ragtime music plays.* **HARRY** *does a strange, vaguely balletic dance. He grunts, makes faces, throws himself around. After just a minute or so, the music comes to an abrupt halt. He again takes his bow.)*

**HARRY.** Thank you, thank you.

**STANFORD.** Not bad, Thaw. But I miss the pas de deux you'd prepared for me and Florence.

**FLORENCE.** It was sublime, wasn't it?

**HARRY.** Good! Back to the script, please. Everyone. Everyone!
**I now call to the stand Mr. Stanford White.**

**EVELYN.** Good luck, Stanny.

**STANFORD.** Thanks, I'm sure. *(Right in front of the stand)* Where, Mr. Thaw?

**HARRY.** Here, here!

*(***STANFORD***, with great difficulty, squeezes himself into the witness stand.)*

**HARRY.** Well I made it myself!

**STANFORD.** You'd never know it...

**HARRY. Now, Mr. Stanford White, would you please state your full name for the court.**

STANFORD. Mr. Stanford White.

HARRY. Stop that! **Mr. White, did you maintain membership at gentlemen's clubs?**

STANFORD. Yes.

HARRY. And what was the general activity at these so-called clubs? Eating?

STANFORD. Yes.

HARRY. Drinking?

STANFORD. Yes.

HARRY. SEX?

STANFORD. Yes.

HARRY. A-HA! **So you were involved in the foul business of illicit sexual practices at these clubs?** With girls, and their little bodies, their tits, their little titties... *(peeling off into some mad, gestural, sick idea of sex)*

STANFORD. Well, it didn't exactly look like that, but—

HARRY. Did you?!

STANFORD. Yes. Hell, I've made no bones about that.

HARRY. That's disgusting! **Mr. White, did you blackball ME from membership in these clubs?**

STANFORD. Bully right I did, you pilfering twit!

HARRY. But I wanted in sooo baaaad...

STANFORD. Thaw, listen to yourself!

HARRY. Not in the script, Stanford.

STANFORD. I don't care. This is insanity!

HARRY. Someone here doesn't know how to handle himself properly in a court of law!

STANFORD. A court of kangaroos!

HARRY. A simple "yes" will do!

STANFORD. No!

HARRY. Yes! I'm getting excited!

EVELYN. Page 12, Harry.

FLORENCE. Hang in there, Stanny!

STANFORD. Hurrah!

HARRY. MR. WHITE, were you considered the taste-maker of your age?

STANFORD. Yes.

HARRY. A man who embodied the essence of turn-of-the-century America, in all its extravagant splendor?

STANFORD. Yes. My, my, Harry, you've done your homework.

HARRY. Thank you. **Were you known to throw lavish, fun-filled parties? With food, and booze,** and girlies, and sex, and little painted chippies with their tits... *(He again peels off into some grotesque version of sex.)*

STANFORD. Yes!

HARRY. That's disgusting! **Mr. White, did you bar MY attendance at these parties?**

STANFORD. Are you hearing what I'm hearing?

HARRY. A yes will do.

STANFORD. **Yes!**

HARRY. Whyyyyy?!

*(STANFORD gestures to him, up and down.)*

HARRY. Stop that! **Mr. White, in the course of your business as an architect did you go on buying trips throughout Europe? Targeting certain estates of the rich just as they were about to go under?**

STANFORD. Yes.

HARRY. **Thereby paying far less than market value for some of the greatest treasures the world had to offer and then selling these furnishings to your American clients at exorbitantly high prices?**

STANFORD. Yes.

HARRY. **Regardless of these underhanded practices and the fact that your clientele roster boasted some of wealthiest families in the world, were you in debt upon your death?**

STANFORD. Yes.

HARRY. **A great deal of debt?**

**STANFORD.** This is getting boring, Thaw.

**HARRY.** Shut up. How much fucking debt?! Go ahead. We both know it's right.

**STANFORD. Five hundred thousand dollars.**

**EVELYN.** What?

**HARRY. Would that translate roughly, in today's currency, to thirteen million dollars?**

**STANFORD. Yes.**

**EVELYN.** That can't be.

**HARRY. Were you the child of a piss poor family?**

**STANFORD. Yes.**

**HARRY. Well, congratulations, Mr. White. There aren't many people I know who could run up a thirteen million dollar tab with absolutely no collateral.**

Hey, I just though of something.

**STANFORD.** What?

**HARRY.** By today's standards, my family could pay off your debt and still have about a billion dollars left over. Pretty good, huh?

**STANFORD.** One billion dollars? That much?

**HARRY.** Probably more. I hear coal's what they now call "global" and let me tell you something - third world labor is one cheap date.

**STANFORD.** I like the sound of that! Let me give you my accountant's card—

**FLORENCE.** Stop! Just stop...This is appalling. You're like a couple of children with toy money to burn. Except, of course, the money is real.

**STANFORD.** Florence, I just admitted to being broke.

**FLORENCE.** Well, you can let your priceless art collection and your huge houses speak for you on that account.

I'm embarrassed to admit I didn't realize just how much money you actually have, Mr. Thaw. *(to* **STANFORD***)* And how much you managed to lose.

When I think of the meals I could have fed my children, the roofs we could have had over our heads.

**STANFORD.** The underwear you could have bought?

**FLORENCE.** Darn right. Do you know how much decent underwear costs? Still, it wouldn't add up to the littlest bit of your millions. Or your billion, was it, Mr. Thaw? Forgive me. I'm sure it's been asked before and by far better people than me, but just how much money does one man need?

**HARRY.** My family made that money fair and square.

**FLORENCE.** On the backs of people like my husband. Like me.

**STANFORD.** Your husband was a lawyer, Florence.

**FLORENCE.** And a very good one, but why do you think we had nothing when he died? Well, I'll tell you, there were only two things you could do in dear old Pittsburgh, Mr. White: work for the people melting steel or the people digging coal.

**HARRY.** So why didn't he?

**FLORENCE.** Because the dumb cluck had what he called "ideals." And look where it left us! Worse off than one of your dollar-a-day employees, Mr. Thaw. I sent my children to bed hungry more nights than not. And barely a bed between us.

**EVELYN.** Do you mean you wish Daddy didn't have ideals?

**FLORENCE.** When you're starving, who can afford them?! …He broke his back defending people against you and your filthy money. And this is what you do with it? You party and philander. You buy more houses and clothes and food than you could ever use. You play. While the people around you drop like flies from coal dust or despair or hunger. What a disgrace.

**EVELYN.** But Mama, we grabbed as much as we could when we had the chance. What does that make us?

**FLORENCE.** Hypocrites, I guess. And squarely part of the, what do they call it, the human condition. I'm sorry for it now. I fear my hands will never come clean.

*(She walks out of the theater. The door slams behind her.* **MIRABELLE** *and* **POIRE** *have come in to the playing*

*area during her speech, for the first time making themselves very present. Without a word,* **STANFORD** *and* **HARRY** *coldly gesture them back to their tables.)*

**HARRY.** Did that make any sense to you?

**STANFORD.** A little.

**EVELYN.** In the 20's, I think they called it Marxism.

**HARRY.** What – like the Marx Brothers?

**STANFORD.** Probably.

**HARRY.** Well, I'm going to take it as a blessing in disguise. An extra bit of surprise drama. Now, back to *my* script. Let's see…**Mr. White, just a few more questions. Did you make it a habit to gain the favor of underage girls?**

**STANFORD. Yes.**

**HARRY. Mr. White, did you make it a habit to drug these girls before you used them or was that just something you did with my Evelyn?!**

**STANFORD.** That's it.

*(He throws his script down and walks out.)*

Florence had the right idea.

**HARRY.** Where are you going?

**STANFORD.** Out to have a cigarette.

**HARRY.** But what about me?

**STANFORD.** Why don't you…go blow it out your ass!

*(Door slams behind him. He's gone.)*

**HARRY.** Well, this leaves me in a bit of a bind. We weren't quite finished with his testimony. Uh…

*(He looks around for a moment, and then hands Stanford's script to a man in the audience.)*

Would you mind? Just there, where it says, "Mr. White, were you in poor health upon your death?" Ready? **Mr. White, were you in poor health upon your death?!**

**MAN.** Yes.

**HARRY. According to an autopsy report, you had a long list of ailments. Is that true?**

MAN. Yes.

HARRY. Tuberculosis?

MAN. Yes.

HARRY. Degeneration of the liver?

MAN. Yes.

HARRY. Disease of the kidneys?

MAN. Yes.

HARRY. High blood pressure?

MAN. Yes.

HARRY. Severe sciatica?

MAN. Yes.

HARRY. Extreme nervousness?

MAN. Yes.

HARRY. Inflammation of the bowels?

MAN. Yes.

HARRY. Did the autopsy report state that you would have died within a year of your death anyway?

MAN. Yes.

HARRY. Then apparently all I did was hasten the inevitable.

MAN. Yes.

HARRY. Thank you. One last question. Mr. White, by standards in place both then and now, were you considered a SEX ADDICT?

MAN. Yes.

HARRY. Disgusting. Mr. White, you may step down! I'll take that now. You read beautifully, thank you.

*(If all goes well, the audience applauds the man's efforts.)*

**There you have it, Ladies and Gentlemen. I'm sure you'll agree that Mr. White here presented the very picture of rotten decay. Partying, profiteering, ill health, addiction. If he didn't deserve to die, who does!?**

Well, I think that was just about flawless. How about you, Evelyn?

*(She throws her script down and walks out.)*

**HARRY.** *(cont.)* Evie? Evelyn!

*(Door slams. She's gone.)*

Well. Luckily, this is where I had planned to sing - all by myself! A little filler music please. Something maternal...

*(The **PIANIST** begins to play as **HARRY** runs behind the drop and produces a music stand. He places himself center stage. When he begins to sing, it is awful, off-key, a fright.)*

When I was sent to jail for avenging the honor of my wife, my dear mother had a number of songs commissioned about my cause. This now, a medley of some of the tunes...

FOR THE SAKE OF A WIFE AND HOME
HE MUST SPEND ALL HIS DAYS ALONE
A LIFE FOR A LIFE IS THE STERN LAW'S DEMAND
UNMERCIFUL LAW WHICH SO FEW UNDERSTAND!

THERE'S A SAD LITTLE WOMAN IN SORROW
WHO FOREVER MUST JOURNEY ALONE
WHILE THE MOTHER OF YEARS PAYS THE COST WITH HER
    TEARS
FOR THE SAKE OF A WIFE AND HOME!

*(Around this point the others begin to come back into the theater, one by one. As he continues to sing, they get progressively obtrusive - talking to each other and the audience, banging the boxing bell, knocking things over. Finally they begin to throw tea cookies at **HARRY**.)*

TWAS A CROWDED ROOF TOP GARDEN
ON A SUMMER'S NIGHT IN JUNE
CHORUS GIRLS UPON THE STAGE
SANG A MERRY TUNE

A SHOT RANG OUT, ALAS!
A SOUL HAD LEFT THIS LIFE
ONE MAN HAD KILLED ANOTHER ONE
BECAUSE HE'D WRONGED HIS WIFE!

WHY DON'T THEY SET ME FREE
GIVE ME MY LIBERTY
JUST BECAUSE I'M A MILLIONAIRE
EVERYONE WANTS TO TREAT ME UNFAIR

MONEY DOES NOT STOP TRUE LOVE
MY ACT PROVED SINCERITY
I DID NOT SHOOT TO SEEK MERE FAME
JUST TO DEFEND MY DEAR WIFE'S NAME

WHY DON'T THEY SET ME FREE
GIVE ME MY LIBERTY—!

*(Someone hits him in the head. The **PIANIST** stops.)*

What the hell is going on here?!

**EVELYN.** Oh, come on Harry. You sang plenty.

**HARRY.** I thought you had all run off and left me alone for the rest of the evening.

**STANFORD.** We considered that, but once we got outside, we were approached by a variety of homeless people asking for cigarettes and money.

*(He lampoons a homeless person, coughing, wheezing, asking for change. It is an embarrassing spectacle, but one he enjoys. He finally winds down.)*

**HARRY.** We seem to be at an uncomfortable impasse, don't we...

Evelyn, it's your turn on the stand. Shall we pick up where we left off?

*(**STANFORD** and **FLORENCE** dissent.)*

**EVELYN.** Hold on. I read ahead in your little script, Harry. And I'm happy to answer any questions you may have - but in my own words.

**HARRY.** *(thinking for a moment)* OK, Boo-fuls.

**FLORENCE.** Where did we go wrong?

**STANFORD.** Coming back in to the theater.

*(**EVELYN** gets on the stand. The others sit.)*

**HARRY.** Mrs. Harry Kendall Thaw, will you please state your full name for the court.

**EVELYN.** Evelyn Nesbit.

**HARRY.** Stop that! **Now, Mrs. Thaw, did you marry me freely and without coercion?**

**EVELYN.** Yes, if you can believe it.

**HARRY.** Your comments are not necessary.

**EVELYN.** Of course they are. I know what you're up to—

**HARRY.** All right! **Now, Mrs. Thaw, throughout our courtship and subsequent marriage, were we known to have fun?**

**EVELYN.** Fun?

**HARRY.** Yes. Parties, good times, restaurants? I took you out a lot, right?

**EVELYN.** I see. Yes, Harry, we had what you would call fun.

**HARRY.** Good. **And throughout our courtship and marriage, did you accept my generous support, financial and otherwise?**

**EVELYN.** What do you mean by otherwise?

**HARRY.** It's a figure of speech, Evelyn. You know, presents and stuff.

**EVELYN.** I took your money if that's what you're getting at.

**HARRY.** That is what I'm getting at. **Finally, Mrs. Thaw, did you on more than one occasion tell me that you loved me?**

**EVELYN.** I did actually.

**HARRY.** A-ha...Ladies and Gentlemen of the court, please note that even when straying from the script the witness here freely admits to enjoying herself with me, to accepting my financial support, and to loving me. Let's see...*(he finds his place)* **And yet, Ladies and Gentlemen, imagine my surprise when I found I had been sold a damaged set of goods!**

**STANFORD.** Here we go again.

**HARRY.** You be quiet. **Evelyn, were you a virgin when I married you?**

**FLORENCE.** This is vulgar!

**EVELYN.** It's all right, mother. No, counselor, I was not a virgin.

**HARRY.** Well, thank you for your candor. **Your mother goes to Pittsburgh and leaves you in the care of the most notorious brute on the eastern seaboard. He takes you to an apartment in the Madison Square Garden. According to your own account, you're drinking with him and suddenly there's a pounding in your ears. It seems the champagne has been drugged! You lose consciousness only to wake up some hours later in bed next to a naked Stanford White!**

**EVELYN.** I know, I wrote it. I wrote a lot of things.

**HARRY.** Well, it's all true…isn't it?

**EVELYN.** Uh…

**STANFORD.** Tell them, Evie. At least tell them I didn't drug you!

**EVELYN.** The problem is I don't know at this point.

**HARRY.** Nonsense.

**EVELYN.** I remember it in many ways. We were drinking. It was late. Maybe I was awake, maybe not. I have a variety of scenarios left over in my head.

**HARRY.** Were you drugged or not?!

**EVELYN.** I don't think so.

**HARRY.** What?!

**STANFORD.** See?! No drugs, no ravishing.

**EVELYN.** Well, that's not necessarily true.

**STANFORD.** Evelyn!

**EVELYN.** Well, Stanny, it's not. I went to your studio that night unawares of the big facts of life and came out the other end shocked and violated.

**HARRY.** A-HA!

**STANFORD.** I didn't make you do anything you didn't want to, young lady. Now that, I remember.

**FLORENCE.** She was sixteen! You were 47 and paying our bills! We trusted you!

**HARRY.** Then it was rape!

**EVELYN.** Of course it was.

**STANFORD.** Evie!

**FLORENCE.** Leave her alone!

**HARRY.** Excellent. Now. **Please tell the court what you did afterwards.**

**EVELYN.** I fell in love with him.

**HARRY.** No, I meant the next morning.

**EVELYN.** Well, Harry, that's not what I meant.

**STANFORD.** Evelyn, leave it be.

**EVELYN.** No. I did. I fell deeply in love with Stanford White. What other choice was there for me?

**HARRY.** Continuing—

**EVELYN.** I am speaking now!

There were only two ways out. Get angry and never speak to Stanford again, which would have left us very hungry and practically homeless. Or – I could embrace the whole situation. Stanford had friends and connections. He found me work and paid our bills. I thought he would marry me.

**STANFORD.** You weren't the only young lady who thought that, my dear.

**EVELYN.** Was I the only one you had to get drunk to lay?

**HARRY.** But you told me he had to drug you.

**EVELYN.** Well at four in the morning, you'll say almost anything. Everywhere, every night. Before we were married and after. Talk, Evelyn, talk. How did he touch you? Where did he touch you? Why did you let him? Tell me again. And again. I made up that story to put an end to it, and look where it got me.

**STANFORD.** Look where it got me.

**EVELYN.** You were the lucky one. I lived!

**HARRY.** Ladies & Gentlemen, she testified at my trial that she was drugged!

**EVELYN.** To save you from the electric chair, Harry!

*(a moment)*

**HARRY.** Continuing. **Mrs. Thaw, was it your habit to mention the name of Stanford White to me often and without provocation?**

EVELYN. No.

HARRY. Oh come on, Evelyn.

EVELYN. Well, I suppose. Occasionally.

HARRY. You were as obsessed as I was.

EVELYN. That's impossible.

HARRY. Infatuated?

EVELYN. No.

HARRY. Fascinated?

EVELYN. No.

HARRY. Hung-up?

EVELYN. All right. Yes, I was hung-up on Stanford.

**HARRY. And Mrs. Thaw, you continued to speak of him even though you knew how the mere mention of his name fueled my murderous rage?**

EVELYN. I brought him up now and again, if that's what you mean.

HARRY. Even though you knew how the *mere mention* of his name fueled my murderous rage!

EVELYN. Yes. Yes, I did.

STANFORD. Evelyn Nesbit!

HARRY. Now we're getting someplace. **Mrs. Thaw, had you heard me threaten to kill Mr. White on more than one occasion?**

*(She says nothing.)*

Had you?!

EVELYN. Yes.

STANFORD. No!

**HARRY. Mrs. Thaw, did you know I was having Mr. White followed?**

EVELYN. Yes.

HARRY. **Mrs. Thaw, did you know that it was my habit to carry a loaded gun?**

EVELYN. Yes.

STANFORD. Evelyn, stop!

HARRY. **Mrs. Thaw, on the night of the murder, did you know that Stanford White was at the same show we were attending on the roof of Madison Square Garden?**

EVELYN. Yes.

HARRY. **Didn't that seem strange to you? The scene of your previous ruination and the man responsible sitting right in harm's way. Certainly you must have known I had a larger plan—**

EVELYN. Yes, I knew! I see what you're trying to do, Harry.

STANFORD. So do I. And I must say thank you, Mr. Thaw. How, Evelyn? How could you let it happen? I took three bullets – in the face!

EVELYN. I didn't pull the trigger!

STANFORD. You might as well have!

EVELYN. You don't have a leg to stand on, you dirty old man. I was raped and shipped off to boarding school.

FLORENCE. Evelyn, please.

EVELYN. You gave your approval every step of the way!

FLORENCE. That's preposterous!

STANFORD. Here here!

EVELYN. I didn't kill you Stanford, but don't think there weren't times when I didn't want to.

HARRY. My point exactly!

EVELYN. And you. Any way you cut it, you end up a murderer.

HARRY. **Ladies and Gentlemen, in summation—**

EVELYN. You know, we haven't heard about you yet, Harry. Anything beyond the poor little rich boy tantrums and the right hooks you planted on me.

HARRY. **In summation—**

**EVELYN.** We didn't hear about your other arrests and convictions. Theft, vandalism, assault. Stanford pales in comparison.

**HARRY.** No, no—

**EVELYN.** How many times did your mother buy off the D.A.? The old lady knew he was dangerous, but did nothing. Except send him back out on the streets over and again with more money and cocaine in his pocket!

**HARRY.** Don't listen—

**EVELYN.** How many times did you promise you'd stop, promise you'd change? As many times as you beat other women?

**HARRY. Harry Kendall Thaw is innocent—**

**EVELYN.** How did it feel when some girl you picked up off the streetpanicked when you came at her with a whip in your hand?

**HARRY.** This isn't going how I'd planned—

**EVELYN.** How did it feel when you turned your violence my way?

**HARRY.** This isn't my script!

**EVELYN.** How did it feel when you raped me?!

**HARRY.** STOP IT. I can not think!

Evelyn...

Put your scripts down. We're going back to the original version. Florence, Stanford, come on!

*(He begins to run around in a panic, pushing things out of the way and gesticulating to the others.)*

**STANFORD.** What, now?

**HARRY.** Yes!

**FLORENCE.** The beginning?

**HARRY.** No, the end of the act. The murder. Just like we rehearsed it. Evelyn, sit down there. You too old man.

*(They arrange their chairs to replicate the rooftop theater. **HARRY** gets his gun and tries to reveal the earlier outdoor courtyard backdrop. It breaks.)*

**HARRY.** *(cont.)* Damn! Play, you. PLAY! Clap everyone, act!

*(The **PIANIST** plays an excited, violent version of "I Could Love A Million Girls." **HARRY** marches toward **STANFORD**, raises the gun and pulls the trigger. It won't go off.)*

Damn!

*(He tries again and again. Click click click.)*

Damn it!

*(Still nothing. He curses and sputters.)*

**STANFORD.** Good night, Irene. *(to the tech booth)* Do you people have a gun-shot noise?

*(A loud BANG BANG BANG fills the room. The music comes to a halt. **STANFORD** goes stiff in his chair and then falls over dead. It looks very real. **EVELYN** screams, throws herself on his body.)*

**HARRY.** I did it, because he ruined my wife!

*(Three boxing bells go off, signaling the end of the act.)*

**HARRY.** Wait. There's more I wanted to tell. This was a fiasco... I'm innocent. Don't you see? Wait. Waaaiiiiit....

*(The lights fade on a chaotic scene. All goes silent. They linger in darkness for a moment.)*

**EVELYN.** Light... please....

*(Lights come up. She's there, still holding **STANFORD**, whose feet are now bare.)*

Good God Harry, what have you done?

That's what I said. Or that's what they said I said. *(to **HARRY**)* They also said I kissed you. Why would I kiss you right now? Maybe I did. I don't know. I have a variety of scenarios left over in my head.

One writer said my life was over that night. But I lived for another 60 years. Sixty. "Stanford was the lucky one. I lived." Ha.

Get up.

*(STANFORD does.)*

You know, I had phenomenal success after all of this happened. After the trials and the public flogging and the very contentious divorce. I sang in clubs all over the country, I broke records in vaudeville, I traveled the world as a star…Until I lost my looks and wasn't one…

I wonder if some of you think this is a joke. At the collective expense of history. At the expense of myself. That's all right. I made my peace long ago. Unlike my friends here, I have no ax to grind. I think…

Well. We haven't done my act yet. And anything can happen.

Go.

## ACT IV – EVELYN'S SHOW

*(The boxing bell fires three loud bangs as a new backdrop is revealed: a beautiful blue sky with white clouds — heaven. A recorded piece of vintage instrumental music plays. Something sexy and tinny with hints of dance hall. After a few bars, Evelyn commands the others.)*

**EVELYN.** 5, 6, 7, 8!

*(The foursome plus* **MIRABELLE** *and* **POIRE** *dance. Throughout the dance* **EVELYN** *orders various of them to clean up the playing area. Occasionally she does a solo turn or special move.)*

*(The dance ends as* **MIRABELLE** *and* **POIRE** *reveal a rolling proscenium unit – a smaller version of the stage proscenium, with a mini grand drape that can be pulled aside for reveals. A red velvet swing appears from the flies and settles center stage.* **EVELYN** *takes a seat in it, framed by the small proscenium. The pianist plays as the others retire.)*

*(***HARRY** *and* **MIRABELLE** *begin drinking. From here on out,* **MIRABELLE** *becomes less and less a servant, and more her own independent figure in the world.* **FLORENCE** *dons a pair of dark glasses and sits in the audience, ostensibly incognito.* **POIRE** *helps* **STANFORD** *to undress.* **EVELYN** *sings.)*

**EVELYN.**
I'M A BROAD-MINDED BROAD FROM BROADWAY
AND CONVENTIONS NEVER BOTHER ME
IF IT'S 4 A.M. WHEN I GET HOME
WHOSE BUSINESS IS IT?

**EVELYN.**
>I'LL SMOKE WHAT I LIKE, AND I LIKE IT!
>IF I'M THIRSTY I'LL DRINK AWAY!
>
>AND IF I FIND MY HUSBAND'S LOVE HAS DIED
>I'LL GO OUT TO THE WOODS AND GET AN INDIAN GUIDE
>I'M A BROAD-MINDED BROAD FROM BROADWAY!
>
>I'M A BROAD-MINDED BROAD FROM BROADWAY
>AND I DON'T CARE WHAT YOU THINK OF ME
>IF IT'S 4 PM WHEN I WAKE UP
>WHOSE BUSINESS IS IT?
>
>I'LL SEE WHO I LIKE WHEN I LIKE TO
>IF I'M LONELY I MIGHT CALL ON YOU
>
>AND IF YOUR LOVE FOR ME HAS FIZZLED OUT
>I'LL HEAD DOWNTOWN TO GET A NEW BOY SCOUT
>I'M A BROAD-MINDED BROAD FROM BROADWAY!

**EVELYN.** Hello, hello, and good evening to everyone. Thank you so very much for coming to the theater tonight…

Welcome to Club Evelyn Nesbit. Maybe we're in Altantic City, maybe we're in Biloxi, maybe we're in Panama. I played – and closed – 'em all!

In the circular mirror of my mind, everyone gets their own act. First I'd like to bring up a fellow who had a pretty rough time of it at the end – but the murder wasn't nothing compared to what happened to him after he died. And here he is: an all-consuming libertine, whose death blew the lid off the bedaubed, bespangled bacchanalia of the upper class – Stanford White!

*(A music shift as **STANFORD**, now half-dressed, produces a piece of colored paper and begins to fold it with great flourish. **POIRE** moves the curtain unit to him, following him as he moves about the stage. Soon **STANFORD**'s paper has become a beautiful origami bird, then another, then another. True magic. He hands them to women in the audience and blows them each a kiss.)*

(**MIRABELLE** *begins to boo. Quietly and intermittently at first, but then she starts to really get in to it.* **FLORENCE** *joins in.* **STANFORD** *decides to try another bit to stem the slow tide of anger coming at him. He pulls out three balls and begins to juggle.* **MIRABELLE** *and* **FLORENCE** *boo louder.*)

**EVELYN.** Stop it!!

(*They do.*)

**EVELYN.** Stanford White was a great man. That he did me wrong does not cloud my judgment. It should not cloud yours…

(**POIRE** *starts hissing, then* **HARRY** *and the other ladies join in. They boo and throw trash at him.* **STANFORD** *juggles faster and faster.* **EVELYN** *tries to out-do the din, to no avail.*)

**EVELYN.** He was a great man! A great man…

(*Chaos. Lights bump up brightly with the elongated sound of feedback and breaking glass. Then an immediate blackout.*)

(*Murky lights fade up on all but* **FLORENCE**, *who is back in the audience, still incognito. The others gently slow dance to a mellow ukulele version of "*Misty.*" After a few moments,* **EVELYN** *speaks.*)

**EVELYN.** As we move forward, let's go back. To the beginning. Here she is: my mother my self, Miss Evelyn Florence Nesbit.

(**FLORENCE** *doesn't come forward from the audience.* **EVELYN** *moves the small proscenium around, providing a frame for someone who isn't there. A follow spot trails around. No* **FLORENCE**.)

**EVELYN.** Mama? Mama?

(*Finally the follow spot finds her.*)

There you are.

**FLORENCE.** (*muttering*) Damn.

**EVELYN.** Come give us a dance or a song.

**FLORENCE.** Do I have to?

**EVELYN.** Please?

**FLORENCE.** It's so safe, here in the audience. Just another member of the great unwashed.

**EVELYN.** *(in a way, asking for all she never got)* Come give us some thing, Mama. Just give us one thing…

*(**HARRY** starts some applause. He holds up a lighter, hoots a bit.)*

*(**POIRE** escorts **FLORENCE** onto the stage and to the small proscenium as music shifts. She does a simple, beautiful dance. **MIRABELLE** moves the curtain around to frame her, more colleague than servant. **EVELYN** happily watches from her swing.)*

*(Meanwhile **POIRE** helps **STANFORD** finish undressing. **HARRY** uses his lighter to burn money, with great aplomb, at his table.)*

*(**FLORENCE**'s dance reaches a crescendo and she takes a bow as the music shifts to a lullaby. She comes to **EVELYN** with a flask. They drink.)*

**EVELYN.** That wasn't so bad, was it?

**FLORENCE.** No. But just so we're clear – I never wanted your stardom for myself. I just wanted something to eat.

**EVELYN.** And a nice pair of drawers.

**FLORENCE.** Who doesn't want that?

**EVELYN.** Hey Mama.

**FLORENCE.** Yes?

**EVELYN.** Remember what you said, after it was all over, when newspapermen would knock on your door in Pittsburgh?

**FLORENCE.** I remember that I didn't remember.

**EVELYN.** Knock. Knock.

**FLORENCE.** Who's there?

**EVELYN.** *(acting a newspaperman)* Stanford White – any comment?

**FLORENCE.** Who?

**EVELYN.** Harry Thaw – any comment?

**FLORENCE.** Who?

**EVELYN & FLORENCE.** *(a jumbled ad-lib)* Stanford who? Harry who? Evelyn who? Who? Who? Who?

*(They chuckle.)*

**EVELYN.** Hey Mama.

**FLORENCE.** Hmm?

**EVELYN.** Why did you leave? You kept leaving.

**FLORENCE.** *(replaying her big moment from the Act I melodrama)* "I find myself society's pawn. The only things I know how to do are raise children and clean house!"

**EVELYN & FLORENCE.** "WHAT SHALL BECOME OF US?!"

*(They laugh and laugh. At his table **HARRY** has begun to laugh too – but with fiendish glee at the spectacle of his burning money. **MIRABELLE** tickles **POIRE**. All are laughing.)*

*(**STANFORD**, now undressed, lies dead upstage, arms folded over his chest and holding a flower, naked but for his underwear. **FLORENCE** suddenly gasps for air and clutches her left arm in horrible pain. She stiffens and falls to the ground.)*

**EVELYN.** Mother? Mama? Mama?!

*(Chaos. Lights bump up brightly with the elongated sound of feedback and breaking glass. Then an immediate blackout.)*

*(Murky lights fade up on **EVELYN** and **HARRY**, **MIRABELLE** and **POIRE** gently slow dancing to "Misty." **FLORENCE** is back in the audience, only now wearing a black shroud. **STANFORD** still lies dead. After a few moments, **EVELYN** walks away from **HARRY**, who then dances by himself.)*

**EVELYN.** And here he is – the most morose, irritable, unhappy creature I ever met. A man who lived and hated life to the fullest, Harry Kendall Thaw – of Pittsburgh!

(**POIRE** *rolls the proscenium in front of* **HARRY** *who is now in wrist and ankle shackles. He performs a Houdini-esque escape act – undoing then re-fastening the cuffs and chains in various combinations with perfect slight-of-hand ease. As* **EVELYN** *narrates, he's free, then in chains, then free again. Circus music accompanies throughout.*)

**EVELYN.** After the murder, the first jury is deadlocked.

**HARRY.** Harry Thaw is a caged man!

**EVELYN.** The second jury finds him not guilty by reason of insanity.

**HARRY.** Harry Thaw is a free man!

**EVELYN.** But the judge sentences him to an insane asylum.

**HARRY.** Harry Thaw is a caged man!

**EVELYN.** The place has almost no security. Harry comes and goes as he pleases.

**HARRY.** Harry Thaw is practically a free man!

**EVELYN.** Finally, several years later, he just walks out, drives to Canada.

**HARRY.** Harry Thaw is a free man – in Canada!

**EVELYN.** Soon after, he's brought back to the U.S. where he's finally judged sane and is released.

**HARRY.** Harry Thaw is a free man – in America!

**EVELYN.** Years later he horse-whips a high school student and is judged insane again.

**HARRY.** Harry Thaw is a caged man!

**EVELYN.** Spends eight more years in an asylum. Finally, he bribes the right judge and is let out one last time.

**HARRY.** Harry Thaw is a free man. For good! Ta-dah! Thank you, thank you!

*(Applause.* **HARRY** *takes a chair and sits next to* **EVELYN** *in her swing. He talks to her as though he's an eager guest on "The Tonight Show." It's his big moment.)*

**EVELYN.** Very handily done, Harry.

**HARRY.** Thank you!

**EVELYN.** Killed a man – at least one we know of – and yet scott free at the end of the day.

**HARRY.** Dementia Americana – fuck 'em, right?

**EVELYN.** You know, aside from the marriage and the murder and the way we both ended up down the crapper, we had all sorts of other things in common.

**HARRY.** Oh yeah?

**EVELYN.** We both had absent fathers.

**HARRY.** My father – dead.

**EVELYN.** Mine too. Completely. And generally less-than-desirable mothers.

**HARRY.** Don't you ever speak ill of my mommy. My mommy loved me.

**EVELYN.** Mine did too, but let's face it, Harry…never mind. After your family left me high and dry, we both entered the motion picture industry.

**HARRY.** Indeed. I tried to make a movie called "The Story of My Life."

**EVELYN.** How'd it go?

**HARRY.** Dismally. No one could get it right. Not even me.

**EVELYN.** I starred in five silent films – all loosely based on the story of my life too!

**HARRY.** Oh yeah?

**EVELYN.** But they're just a pile of dust now. Film, as it turns out, doesn't last. You and me, puppets bound by the inexorable hand of fate, will go on forever.

**HARRY.** Sure.

**EVELYN.** You know what else we had in common? Morphine and cocaine.

**HARRY.** You partake?

**EVELYN.** I've managed to reduce my requirement to a small dose, but admit I can not dislodge the craving altogether.

**HARRY.** You want a bump?

**EVELYN.** Why not?

*(He searches through his pockets, finds his gun which he nonchalantly puts in her hands. Then he finds a little kit of works and a vial. She pockets the gun and does a line, while he preps a syringe.)*

And one last shared pursuit: our child.

**HARRY.** He wasn't mine.

**EVELYN.** Yes he was.

**HARRY.** No he wasn't.

**EVELYN.** Yes he was.

**HARRY.** No he wasn't.

**EVELYN.** Harry, the boy I had was yours.

**HARRY.** *(a true admission)* All right, he was.

**EVELYN.** *(finally, a wrong is righted)* Thank you.

*(**EVELYN** does another line, while **HARRY** continues with his syringe.)*

**HARRY.** Listen, about that - I want to give you something before I kick off.

*(He hands her a wad of cash.)*

This, my dear, is ten thousand dollars. A gift in my will.

**EVELYN.** Thank you, Harry. You know what I'm gonna do with this? Give it to Emma Goldman.

**HARRY.** Who's Emma Goldman?

*(A beat. She chuckles at him not knowing.)*

**EVELYN.** One of the Marx Brothers.

*(The drugs have kicked in for them both. He gently falls back as she ramps up. Meanwhile, **STANFORD** and **FLORENCE**, both dead, make out elsewhere in the theater. **POIRE** has gotten a hold of **MIRABELLE** and is putting the moves on her too. He tries to kiss her, grab her. Is it playful? No. She finally slaps his face and gets free.)*

**EVELYN.** Oh and one last thing...

**HARRY.** What's that?

**EVELYN.** Now that I think of it, we both...were in love... with Stanford White!

*(Chaos. Lights bump up brightly with the elongated sound of feedback and breaking glass. Then an immediate blackout.)*

*(Murky lights fade up on **MIRABELLE**, **POIRE**, and **EVELYN**, gently slow dancing, to "Misty." **FLORENCE**, **HARRY** and **STANFORD**, now all dead, chat with each in a corner somewhere. After a few beats, **EVELYN** gently speaks.)*

Ladies and Gentlemen, I'd like to bring someone back to the stage who, I feel, didn't quite get the reception he deserves. Benevolent vampire, fashionable degenerate, apostle of beauty. Not just King, but creator of New York – Stanford White...

*(He comes to her. Holds her. They dance, speaking quietly, affectionately. During the following, **MIRABELLE** changes in to contemporary dress.)*

**EVELYN.** You were the only man I ever loved.

**STANFORD.** You, my dear, made me shiver with delight.

**EVELYN.** Thank you...

I didn't pull the trigger.

**STANFORD.** You might as well have.

**EVELYN.** No. All you had to do was let Harry in to your club. I let him in to mine.

**STANFORD.** I forgive you any way.

**EVELYN.** Oh, Stanny. You always knew how to make me laugh...

Imagine if I hadn't met you. If the greed and lust and confused energy of an entire age hadn't played themselves out on me. Imagine further if I had not been

**EVELYN.** *(cont.)* just left alone, but, instead, had been nurtured and cared for and allowed to become my highest best self. Imagine me then! I blame you for nothing. You simply made a way for me. A painful way, yes. But a way that was solely and inevitably mine. And you know what I did with that way? I lived. I'm so grateful to have lived!

*(He lets her go and opens his arms wide. She has Harry's gun. She shoots. He falls gently to the ground. A dance move.)*

**EVELYN.** *(sweetly, as though she were tucking him in to bed)* Good night. You glamorous thief.

*(She sits in her swing, alone. She sings.)*

YOU MAY WONDER WHAT'S THE REASON FOR THIS CRAZY SMILE
I'M HAPPY, HAVEN'T BEEN SO HAPPY IN A LONG WHILE
GOT A LOAD OFF MY MIND, I'M FEELING FINE…

I CAN COME WHEN I PLEASE, I CAN GO WHEN I PLEASE
I'M A GIRL WHO CAN FLIRT, TANTALIZE AND TEASE
BECAUSE I'M NO MAN'S WOMAN NOW

I CAN SAY WHAT I LIKE, I CAN DO WHAT I LIKE
I'M A SINGLE GIRL ON MATRIMONIAL STRIKE
BECAUSE I'M NO MAN'S WOMAN NOW

I CAN SMILE, I CAN WINK, I CAN GO TAKE A DRINK
AND I DON'T HAVE TO WORRY WHAT MY LOVER WILL THINK
BECAUSE I'M NO MAN'S WOMAN NOW!

*(Finally, she begins to use her swing, swaying upstage and down.* **MIRABELLE** *watches for a moment then leaves the theater, crossing through the house.* **POIRE**, *ever the servant, begins to clean up the stage as* **HARRY**, *then* **STANFORD**, *then* **FLORENCE** *push* **EVELYN**.*)*

Higher. Higher. Higher…

*(Lights bump up brightly then slowly fade.)*

**END OF PLAY**

# ACKNOWLEDGEMENTS

I'm grateful to the many people who were instrumental to the writing and production of the play. My sincere thanks to the various casts who helped me discover and hone the script throughout its many processes (especially the world premiere cast), to the organizations who helped me develop the work: the Indecent Exposure Theater Company, the City of Los Angeles Cultural Affairs Department and the Mark Taper Forum, and to my colleagues and students at Occidental College.

Thanks to Chris Wells and Tracy Young for reviewing the manuscript before publication, to Curtis Heard for his generosity and support in preparing the music and contributing original lyrics and music, and to Claudia Gomez for her cover art. Deep gratitude to Jabez Zuniga who was instrumental to this publication.

I am indebted to a variety of research sources. Primary thanks go to Professor Paula Uruburu of Hofstra University, the acknowledged expert on Evelyn Nesbit. Her insights via interview were invaluable in fashioning the original script. Thanks to her also for sharing copies of the Thaw songs. Her wonderful book *American Eve* was an inspiration when re-visiting the script for publication.

Other helpful sources were Evelyn's memoirs *The Story of My Life* and *The Untold Story*, *Stanford White's New York* by David Lowe, *The Architect of Desire* by Suzannah Lessard, *Evelyn Nesbit and Stanford White* by Michael Macdonald Mooney, *The Girl in the Red Velvet Swing* book by Charles Samuels and film by Walter Reisch and Charles Brackett, the novel *Ragtime* by E.L. Doctorow, and the reporting of the *Los Angeles Times* and the *New York Times*.

## LYRIC AND MUSIC CREDITS

All of the songs were chosen either for their direct relation to the story or for their historical resonance. The songs from Act I premiered in reviews then went on to become part of the vaudeville repertoire. The original *I Could Love A Million Girls* was making its debut performance when Stanford was shot in the audience. The numbers in Act II are representative of the some of the major themes in popular songs of the day: charming philanderers and sainted mothers, school pride and romantic zeal. Harry's Act III songs were indeed commissioned for him by his mother. Evelyn's songs in Act IV were from her post-trial cabaret act. Only lyrics could be found – the music has been lost to time.

Choral arrangements are by Curtis Heard.

"I Could Love a Million Girls"
from the 1906 review *Mam'zelle Champagne*
chorus refrain lyrics by Edgar Allan Woolf
all other lyrics by Laural Meade
music by Cass M. Freeborn

"Oh By Jingo"
from the 1919 review *Linger Longer Letty*
gibberish lyrics by Lew Brown
all other lyrics by Laural Meade
music by Albert Von Tilzer

"Heaven Will Protect the Working Girl"
from the 1909 review *Tillie's Nightmare*
chorus lyrics by Edgar Smith
all other lyrics by Laural Meade
music by A. Baldwin Sloane

"Who Are You With Tonight?"
1910
lyrics by Harry Williams
music by Egbert Van Alstyne

"Thee, Pamlico"
from the 1902 collected works *Songs of All the Colleges*
arranged and compiled by David Chamberlain and Karl Harrington

"Your Mother is Your Best Friend"
1914
lyrics and music by Charles Coleman

"Am I Not Fondly Your Own?"
from the 1902 collected works *Songs of All the Colleges*
arranged and compiled by David Chamberlain and Karl Harrington

"For The Sake of a Wife and Home"
1906 commission by the Thaw family
lyrics by Ross Edward
music by Fred Leopold

"Why Don't They Set Him Free"
1906 commission by the Thaw family
lyrics by Thomas J. Blue
music by Harry C. Loll

"Broadminded Broad from Broadway"
from Evelyn's nightclub repertoire
1st stanza lyricist unknown
2nd stanza lyrics by Curtis Heard
music by Curtis Heard

"No Man's Woman Now"
from Evelyn's nightclub repertoire
lyricist unknown
music by Curtis Heard

# OTHER TITLES AVAILABLE FROM SAMUEL FRENCH

## 27 RUE DE FLEURUS (MY LIFE WITH GERTRUDE)

### Ted Sod & Lisa Koch

*Musical / 5f /Unit Set*

Unlike most of the stage works about Gertrude and Alice, *27 Rue de Fleurus* is told from Alice's point of view. Gertrude grows tired of Alice's lack of panache for telling her perspective of their story and attempts to hijack the play as only the author of such lines "sugar is not a vegetable" can. But Alice has secrets to share with the audience that silence the famously verbose Gertrude. This celebrated couple confronts each other about love, marriage, jealousy, genius and a few other delicious topics while Pablo Picasso, F. Scott Fitzgerald, Mabel Dodge, Sylvia Beach and even Jean Harlow drop by for a visit.

"*27 Rue de Fleurus* gets its sweetness from a genuine love of its subject, the "marriage" of Gertrude Stein and Alice B. Toklas. The music is well handled by John Bell; and the all-female cast sings excellently."
– *The Village Voice*

"What we have here is a love story, fraught with jealousy and passion like others, but most of all, it celebrates the incredible bond between two women who decided to share their lives, even during a time when it was relatively unheard of. That alone makes *27 Rue de Fleurus* worth an evening of your time."
– *GO Magazine*

"Ms. Rosenblat, who, seated, resembles portraits of Stein, plays Gertrude as a commanding bully. And Ms. Stern's Alice is a bright, attractive creature. ("Everyone is entitled to a bit of fantasy," she says.) They're strong, plausible performances."
– *The New York Times*

SAMUELFRENCH.COM

# OTHER TITLES AVAILABLE FROM SAMUEL FRENCH

## THE BEAUX' STRATAGEM

Adapted by Thornton Wilder and Ken Ludwig
From the Play by George Farquhar

*Comedy / 8m, 5w, with doubling / Various Locations*

The play tells the story of two young bucks who, having spent all their money by living too well, leave London and roam from town to town in search of love and fortune. In order to find a wealthy heiress for at least one of them, they pose as master and servant – exchanging roles from one town to the next. In Lichfield, Aimwell is the master and Archer the servant, and there they meet the lovely, wealthy Dorinda and her equally desirable sister-in-law, Mrs. Kate Sullen. They set their caps for these women, but problems abound. Kate is married to a drunken sot who despises her; the innkeeper's saucy daughter, Cherry, has set her cap for Archer; Dorinda's mother, Lady Bountiful, mistakenly believes herself to be a great healer of the sick, and she guards her daughter like a dragoness; and a band of brigands plans to rob the house of Lady Bountiful that very night, putting all schemes in jeopardy. This is a play in the great tradition of Goldsmith's *She Stoops to Conquer* and Sheridan's *The Rivals* and *The School for Scandal*. It is classic, formal, robust and hilarious.

"A delightful romp ... A sparklingly funny evening that... plays very well indeed."
– *Potomac Stages*

"A sparkling production ... The dialogue crackles, the characters engage the audience's interest and sympathy, and the whole thing seems almost effortless."
– *Talkinbroadway.com*

SAMUELFRENCH.COM

# OTHER TITLES AVAILABLE FROM SAMUEL FRENCH

## EMILIE: LA MARQUISE DU CHÂTELET DEFENDS HER LIFE TONIGHT

### Lauren Gunderson

*Historic/Docu Drama / 2m, 3f*

Passionate. Brilliant. Defiant. Tonight, 18th century scientific genius Emilie du Châtelet is back and determined to answer the question she died with: love or philosophy, head or heart? In this highly theatrical rediscovery of one of history's most intriguing women, Emilie defends her life and loves; and ends up with both a formula and a legacy that permeates history.

"Gunderson possesses an antic imagination that seeks to invent its own rules. As soon as we're drawn in, she shakes us and whisks us 10 or 15 paces ahead."
– *Los Angeles Times*

"The ambitious, non-linear experiment is a highly theatrical romp that literally crackles with electricity."
– *LA/OC Examiner*

SAMUELFRENCH.COM

# OTHER TITLES AVAILABLE FROM SAMUEL FRENCH

## WEST MOON STREET

Rob Urbinati

*Comedy / 4m, 4f, possible doubling / Unit Set*

Young Lord Arthur is deliriously happy – just down from Oxford and engaged to be married – when a mysterious palm reader predicts that he will commit a murder. A proper English gentleman, Arthur believes it is his Duty to get this killing business over with before he marries. But his education has not provided him with the required skills, and a hilarious series of mishaps ensues as he sets about finding a victim.

"Oscar Wilde's short story *Lord Arthur Savile's Crime* is a clever mystery, written to indict the fate industry with whom late-19th-century aristocrats seemed so enthralled. The writer Rob Urbinati has molded the story into a briskly paced comedy of manners true to its author's greater spirit. A complete delight!"
– *The New York Times*

"Urbinati's adaptation is deft, using the source material to its fullest and beautifully fleshing out several minor characters only alluded to in the original story."
– *Backstage*

"Rob Urbinati has done a truly marvelous thing: He's turned an infrequently read Oscar Wilde short story into a play that improves on the original. A Wilde ride indeed!"
– *The New York Blade*

SAMUELFRENCH.COM

www.ingramcontent.com/pod-product-compliance
Lightning Source LLC
Chambersburg PA
CBHW071410290426
44108CB00014B/1765